THE EVE FACTOR
Strengthening The Male-Female Relationship

THE EVE FACTOR

Strengthening The Male-Female Relationship

STEVE B WALTERS

Crowned Warrior Publishing
Norcross, GA 30092

The Eve Factor – Strengthening The Male-Female Relationship

© 2005 Steve B. Walters

ISBN: 978-0-9719767-1-9

1st printing 2005

All scripture quotations are taken from the Authorized King James
Version of the Bible.

Editor: Anthony Buissereth

Cover Design: Scott Lester

Publisher: Crowned Warrior Publishing

Author's Website: www.stevewaltersministries.com

Published in the United States of America

TABLE OF CONTENTS

WHAT IS THIS BOOK ABOUT?

This book talks about how females tend to give so much of themselves particularly to the males in their lives until there is nothing left for self. It further discusses the dangers, blessings and opportunities it presents to both males and females. Finally it provides them tools to better understand each other, resolve their issues and develop deeper and more meaningful familial relationships.

DEDICATION

This book is dedicated to three very dear and influential people in my life:

First my mom Sarah Walters for being such a patient and loving wife who believed that her husband could be much more than he ever thought he could. You demonstrated to me what a wife should be.

Secondly my late Aunt Margree Howard who talked and counseled me about females for what seemed 24 hours a day. She was always instructing and warning me of the pitfalls much like King Lemuel's mom (Proverbs 31). You taught me to search for the beautiful treasure within every female. I dearly miss our conversations and friendship.

And finally in memory of my dad Thomas Paul Butler who constantly talked to me about becoming a good husband, father, treating a female with respect and was determined that I would become a one-woman man. Dad I am pleased to tell you that the one woman I've been married to greatly appreciates your teaching and reports that your efforts were not in vain.

ACKNOWLEDGEMENTS

Family

To my personal "Eve", Sharon Victoria Walters, I am so glad that you are my wife and yet you are so much more. You are friend, confidant, prophetess, advisor, secretary, lover, mistress and my "Extra Special Love." You are the one for whom I've been waiting all of my life! Thanks for being the good woman behind the good man.

My oldest daughter Katrina Denise Walters (Coco), you have been a great help in the writing of this book. I truly enjoyed and hold dear the time we were able to spend together. I am so proud of the woman you are and are yet becoming. Thanks for allowing me to use your picture for the original cover of this book. You know your daddy loves you!

To my only son Steven Butlerson Walters, I am confident in the man within you, proud of the courage you possess and grateful for your ability and daring to dream. I am thankful to my Lord Jesus that I am your father and you are my son.

To Jenjen, Jenise La Vonne Walters, the end of my strength, the world has yet to behold the blessing you are destined to be. You are so multitalented. It is a great honor to have you contribute to this book. (And then there's ......) (Are you my.....) You know exactly what I'm talking about.

To my grandsons Dorian (Shemei), Malik (Judah) and Tre (Michaiah): No grandfather could love or be prouder of his grandchildren than I am of you. I love you boys. We will build an empire together.

To the best Mother-In-Law in the whole world (Ms Vernice Tomblin); your continuous prayers for me have been a source of comfort, encouragement and blessing over my life. I am grateful for the love you have shown me through the years. Thank you again for giving birth to the mother and grandmother of my children and for encouraging her to choose me.

Aunt Annie Mae Thames you always said I could do it. Thank you so much for a listening ear and believing in me.

My Wonderful Eves

Coretta Youmans: Thanks for allowing me to totally wear you out with my enthusiasm about this book and for going with me on so many interviews when my wife was unable.

A special thanks goes to the many wonderful ladies who gave of their time to make sure that the information gathered was accurate and suitable from a female perspective. Some of them are Veronica Miller, Karen Tatum, Gerri Black, Cynthia Nelson, Kimberly De Reuter, Teena Stotts, Veronica Pless, Tesa Johnson, Latisha (Tee-tee) Kornegay, Teresa Hodge, Katrina Walters, Lynn Beals, Jenise Walters and a host of ladies who's names I never knew or cannot remember due to meeting them either on a plane, train or in passing. I am so grateful for your time and input.

I especially send out a big hug and special thanks to all of the lovely ladies who were so willing to be interviewed.

This book would not exist without you. Your input is so appreciated. You know who you are.

The Brothers

To all of the brothers out there of all ages who have assisted me by sharing their knowledge and taking the time to have discussion groups over these and many other issues, I owe you a debt of gratitude. Thanks for being true men who love their wives, take care of their families, have a genuine desire to have meaningful relationship with the females in their lives with the determination to do whatever it takes. I salute you and sing your praises in spite of the fact that so many say that we do not exist.

My Coaches And Cheerleaders @ Suntrust

Mark Ausmus *(Head Coach)*, Brenda Tuggle, Bruce Hopkins, Denise Johnson, Richard Jones, Audrey Davis, Rafael Brito, Unsal Sunay, Stephen Noble, Theodore Tarver, Bruce Stevens, Bob Andrew, Norm Small, Eveleen Harrison, David Cowart, Bill Cheeley, Jay Davis, Hin-Lee Tang, Rick O'Dom, Tim Coveney, Chris Maughan, Karen (Catwoman) Jones, Pat Robinson, Lee Boise, Joann Neeley, Carolyn Dunn, Lisa Klenzak, Lisa Zembower, Larry Zwettler, Kevin Chichon, Andy Dunn & Pat Frain.

Editing

Anthony you haven't even scratched the surface of what I know you are capable of. I get so excited when I look at what you've already done. Thank you so much for your diligent efforts of making this book what it is and will become.

Finally to our many well wishers whose names are far too many to mention, we are grateful to you for being the wind

14

beneath our wings and for that we thank you from the
depths of our hearts

Uses For This Book

It is our intention that readers use this book on numerous forums and a multiplicity of ways to strengthen individuals, their relationships with the opposite sex and the healing of broken lives. While it may not have all of the answers it is certainly an excellent place to start. For this reason it is written in such a manner that it can be used in the following ways:

- Pre-Marital/Post Marital Counseling
- As part of an abused women program
- Basic Relationship Training
- Women's/Men's Ministry
- Single's Ministry
- Ministerial Training
- In schools to teach teens appreciation and for the opposite sex
- As a wedding present
- Self Improvement
- Present to a male friend or relative
- Present to a female friend or relative

PREFACE

There I was approaching the gate to Aunt Margree's house; it had been quite a while since we've spent time together. Aunt Laura, Uncle Howard and my cousin Vernetta were also waiting for me to arrive. It was going to be so great to see them again. I was so excited that I leaped over some of the stairs on my way to the door. Landing on the top step I rang the front door bell. There she was with a big smile filled with so much love that you could feel it embrace you through the door.

"Hi Aunt Marg," I said. As usual she gave me the biggest embrace, told me that she loved me, how happy she was to see me and how handsome she thought I was. No sooner than stepping into the living room from the front enclosed porch and saying hi to everyone, Aunt Marg said, "Stevie, I need to tell you something!"

We immediately went to her room and she told me to sit down. Not knowing what she had on her mind I was looking at her wondering if it was bad news or if there was something I had unwittingly done.

"Stevie" she proclaimed, "when a female tells you what she is going to do and what she is not going to do after she marries you and laughs about it, she means it! Stevie, she means it. She means it, Stevie!" This is typical of the information that Margree Howard, my dear aunt, would make sure I understood. My Aunt Marg, as many of us affectionately referred to her, was one of my best friends. She and I would talk for hours about life and especially about females. It was important to her that I develop into the type of man that not only loved females but one that had a deep appreciation for what a female brought to the table within a relationship. For this reason, plus the fact that we loved each other so much, we spent a lot of time together. Unfortunately Aunt Marg was often very sick but her drive and outlook on life was one of the most exciting things about her. For it gave her a spark that caused you to think and feel that this woman could not possibly be as physically sick as you knew she actually was. She always taught us that we should settle for nothing but the best and displayed it in everything she did. I have been so inspired by the way she would go out to work (when she really should not be working at all) just so that she could totally redo her home in the fashion that a Butler (her maiden name) is accustomed to. She was, as she would put it, all female and proud of it. The knowledge she shared with me has been extremely invaluable in all of my relationships with females. They have caused some to be very short and others very rewarding. Mostly it has taught me how to become good friends with females. While Aunt Margree was schooling me on the treasures within all females her brother (my dad), Elder Thomas Paul Butler was determined that I would never become a playboy or in today's vernacular a "PLAYER".

He talked quite a bit about marriage and how fortunate a man is when he has found a wife. He made sure that I understood the difference between a female and a wife. I remember days when we would be talking about certain situations and he would say things like "She is not a wife! She may be married, but she is certainly not a wife!" On the other hand, he would talk to me about how to appreciate a wife. I remember so clearly how he used to tell me "Stevie, you've got to put woman in a house. An apartment is all right for a short time, but you need to put a wife in a house. A wife is not quite settled until she is in her own house. She needs to be able to change it and decorate it so that it will reflect her taste without worrying if anyone will disapprove of her making them." He also explained that when I get the house that it would not be mine. Oh yes I would have to pay for it, but it would be her house. He'd talk to me about having a family and being a provider for them. He said that being a man is more than bringing home the bacon and that it was extremely important for you to be a father to a child and not just the father of the child. These things he would talk about with great intention, always describing them as a blessing and not a chore.

My mother, Sarah Walters on the other hand, was actually demonstrating the picture of what my dad Thomas had been teaching me. She truly loved my father, Allen, as she called him, and took excellent care of him. But don't get it twisted; my mom was nobody's pushover. She is a woman that stood up for self. You were not going to lay a finger on her without pulling back a nub. Nevertheless the way that she would prepare his meals, lay out his clothes and tolerate some of the things he did, said to me that she really loved him. In addition to this my mom always told me stories about her dad, how great a man he was, the wonderful relationship she enjoyed with him and how grateful he was when she and my dad had to come back home to him. I have been blessed with some great examples through these people.

My dad also had such great friendships with his sisters Margree, Tootsie, Laura and Larfaye. They laughed, talked, argued, made up and were sure to converge at Grandma Butler's house for Mother's Day and especially Thanksgiving. I remember him saying to my Aunt Marg after she had made him a sandwich with the bread toasted just the way he liked it, the napkin folded ever so neatly and a nice cup of coffee brewed to perfection; "Margree you make the best sandwiches!" She replied to him, "I do, Chuck?" He then said, "Yes, because you make your sandwiches with a lot of love." Wow! That still gets to me.

Can you imagine how she felt about her brother and how he felt about his sister? I remember working in the kitchen with my surrogate mom Ernestine Watts. She is one of the best cooks in the world but don't look at the kitchen after she is done. Believe me it is totally wrecked when she's finished. In an effort to keep from having a humongous mess to clean up afterwards, I would sometime clean as she cooked. It was customary for us to have some of the best mother-son talks while preparing a major (and I did say major) meal. I remember so clearly her saying to me, "Stevie, when you have a wife you must always let her know that she is appreciated. Let her know that you enjoyed the meal she took the time to cook for you and compliment her on how she looks regardless of how much weight she may or may not gain. These things are important to a woman."

I must say, all of these influences have richly blessed my life and have allowed me to have the most amazing friendships with females. Of course some were not so wonderful because having friendships with a female who is not a relative can sometimes turn into unrequited love. In most cases, when that occurs the friendship is over.

Nevertheless, as I look back over my life, these friendships have allowed me to prepare for the most rewarding female friend of all; the one I now am privileged to enjoy with my lovely wife Sharon Victoria Walters. After getting to know me and as well as meeting some of my relatives my wife told me that I did all of the right things without knowing it. She also said that she needed to help me learn to tone it down. Believe me I had no idea that being a gentlemen could get you into so much trouble. You see I had been brought up to treat females with respect. I was, as I often refer to it, brainwashed into being a gentlemen. Its unfortunate boys aren't taught this today. I was taught that you do not hit a female; you protect, hold the door open for, pull out a chair for and love them. You know I have been giving biblical advice to couples for over twenty-seven years and the most rewarding thing that I have experienced is seeing them, their children and their relationships blossom. There is no match for that; it is in a class all by itself.

It is from this background that I have come to write this book. While I believe that the husband and wife relationship is the ultimate relationship between males and females, I am also very much concerned with all of the others as well. The truth is each and every one of them is vital to us. I get tired of seeing so many with such great potential hidden within their treasure boxes lose to so many insignificant issues. Insignificant in that they are small compared to what can be achieved if they fight to build and search for the treasure within. I am keenly aware of the many problems that plague our relationships and am not pretending to cover all of them in this book, but am attempting to contribute to the success of all male-female relationships by bringing to light one phenomenon that is common to them all regardless to the type of male-female familial association it is. I believe that brothers and sisters, mothers and sons, fathers and daughters, uncles and nieces and of course nephews and aunts will benefit from what is contained within these pages. So come on let's get started exploring what I like to call "The Eve Factor."

SECTION ONE

THE EVE FACTOR

CHAPTER ONE

WHAT IS THE EVE FACTOR?

The "Eve Factor" is about how females tend to give so much of themselves to the males in their lives until there seems to be nothing left. We find that once they arrive at the point where they've given all, they continue to give. This continuous "pouring out" phenomenon is what we refer to as her being lost. It is sometimes referred to as "losing your Self." The fact that a female can go from one extreme, being a tower of strength in the life of a male, and then suddenly become someone who is totally helpless doesn't seem to be logical to most males and can be a source of major problems.

Why do you think males end up saying or doing the wrong things when she needs him to be more sympathetic and helpful to her the most? It is because of a lack of information, training and is affected by life experiences. I am not asking females to understand or accept this fact, but am only suggesting that you become aware of it. By the same token I am not trying to fully explain females to males, but rather attempting to arm males with some tools to better their relationships with the females in their lives.

The "Eve Factor" also includes the many other ways in which this affects the male-female relationship. While we will be discussing some negative things we will also focus on the positive. The idea here is to ·strengthen the male-female relationship. The goal is to inform, empower and improve relationships through the dissemination of information. As you can see, this is not limited to romantic relationships between males and females but is relevant to all male-female relationships. In this book, however, we will primarily focus on relationships with those we have a familial connection. While there are probably thousands of issues/complexities within any male-female relationship and many more books that deal with them, it is our determination to focus on one.

"The Eve Factor" is not a true relationship issue within itself but a normal experience from which many issues arise. I am a firm believer that God intended that males and females were meant to get along, partner with one another and have great success together. I believe this in spite of the difficulties and differences we have. I believe it regardless of the harmful blending of genders in today's world, the divorce rate, the decline in teaching respect for the female, the garbage we call entertainment (where women are depicted as pure sex objects to be used at the whim of any male who has an urge and particularly their portrayal on television commercials, movies and children's cartoons).

I say if you want to destroy a nation of people, you need to destroy the males, but if you want to destroy the moral fiber of a nation and cause it to become self destructive, then you must reduce and defile the worth of the female. When we look at the problems we are having in our nation it can easily be traced in some way to these two things. I was taught growing up that the best thing you will ever do for your children is to love their mother. I am tired of hearing of so many couples being defeated in their relationships and succumbing to the trap of speaking negative about each other only to finally end up treating each other in a manner that will only lead to disease. In the course of reading this book there will be terminology that we feel needs clarification. Some of it is necessary because it is clearly understood from either a male or female perspective while the other sex may not. For this reason we will take the time to make them clear. As you read them keep in mind that the object of discussing them is to recognize, appreciate, become more in tune with and benefit from these differences. With that thought in mind let's get started.

LOSING YOURSELF

We are keenly aware of the fact that females do not only experience this with the males in their lives, however, for this book we are primarily focusing on the male-female relationship as it relates to this phenomenon. What exactly do we mean when we say she has lost herself? Obviously we are not speaking in the literal sense of being physically lost but rather a spiritual/emotional state of being lost. It is sort of like giving your all and, in spite of having nothing left, everyone is expecting you to be at your best. You just cannot function properly. Think of it as her losing her sense of wholeness or better yet think of her walking around feeling incomplete with no idea of why she is experiencing it or, for that matter, how she arrived at this point. Actually, in many cases, females do not know that they've lost themselves until they've been there for quite some time. It is my intention to help them and the males in their lives recognize when this occurs, learn what to do to help her find herself again and thereby strengthen the relationship between them. In an effort to help females better recognize when they are there as well as give you a better idea of what they may be going through, we have compiled the following list:

When a female is what we call "lost" she may:
- Feel as if she has no direction
- Feel as if she no longer knows who she is as a person is in this world or where she belongs
- Feel that her life has no meaning and she has not accomplished anything in her life when in reality she has made many meaningful contributions and accomplishments
- Think that she is not contributing to the relationship/household when all she has done is contribute
- Feel that the male in her life is using and taking advantage of what she contributes to the relationship as opposed to being one who is appreciative and grateful for it
- Feel totally unappreciated and used up
- Have no clue as to what is wrong
- Not be able to tell you what is wrong
- Be quite angry, moody, frustrated and misunderstood (without PMS)
- Feel undeserving of good
- Be an abused woman who is not willing to admit to herself that things are wrong and she deserves better
- Be unable or unwilling to admit that she is being used and is settling for much less than she should
- Find herself consistently doing things that benefit or make others happy and very little or anything that benefit or make themselves happy

Ladies, if you are experiencing any combination of these things, then take some time for introspection because you may very well have lost your self. It may be time for replenishment. I understand your need to feel a sense of accomplishment or purpose, but at this point you need to take the time to look back over your life and realize what meaningful things you have already done. Sometimes you need to simply remember what made you happy prior to your present situation. The main thing, however, is replenishment.

HE DOESN'T KNOW SHE'S LOST

Contrary to some feminine belief most males, unfortunately, are not aware that females go through this experience. They know that something is going on, but don't know what it is. Even when they see it, they don't know what they are looking at and often end up responding to it in an improper manner. From a male perspective it is viewed as a female going through one of those crazy emotional episodes again. Have you ever heard males say, "We can't live with them and we can't live without them?" Well that's how they view it. Have you noticed that some get so frustrated and resign themselves to giving up on understanding women? Why do they come to this point? It is because males think that they have to fix things and when they see the "Eve Factor" it doesn't make any sense because of the perceived contradictions in the female's actions.

The truth is males think differently from females and when a female goes through something like the "Eve Factor" it is like someone just turned on a foreign language television station; they don't understand what's being communicated. For example, females think that males always know when something is wrong, but they don't.

How many times has a female been angry with a male for something he has or has not done and he looks at her and says, "What's wrong?" Of course at that point she gives him the cold shoulder, a blank stare, looks of disgust or answers him with the proverbial, "You know what's wrong!" Then he stands there with a look of pure confusion mixed with frustration and guilt over something he feels totally clueless about. At this point he realizes that he must have done something wrong. He now proceeds to try to get some answers by asking what may be perceived in her mind as a stupid question: "Do you want to talk about it?" To which she answers "NO!" What does he do then? Picture this without sound. We are all familiar with what he is saying. I do not have to repeat it here, but picture this. His hands fly up in the air, his face displays a very clear sign that says "FORGET IT, I GIVE UP, I SURRENDER, I QUIT" and he turns in the opposite direction and proceeds to move as far away from her as humanly possible. At this point she is totally ticked off because he didn't understand that her "NO" was in reality a "YES" that said you need to pursue me and show me that I'm worth fighting for.

Now be honest. Does this scenario sound familiar to you? We'll get into the way we communicate in a later chapter, but for now please understand that most men do not know when a woman has lost herself. Therefore, in an effort to help them better recognize when she is there we have the following list of signs (in addition to what we've already mentioned) for him to watch for:

- She's lost that sense of independence and confidence about herself (in spite of how she looks or what she is achieving)
- Constantly asking if you love her
- She needs much more of your time and attention than usual (needy/clingy) may be overly possessive or jealous

- She doesn't seem to be taking special time for herself (check the grooming)
- She can't seem to get motivated or make decisions for herself
- You ask what's wrong and she doesn't know
- You try to solve her problem and she gets frustrated and upset about it
- She's constantly getting frustrated with you (more than usual)
- She seems to be accusing you of using and abusing what she does in the relationship as opposed to being thankful for and appreciating it
- She doesn't think you care or understand her regardless to what you do

If you are seeing a combination of these signs, there is a great possibility that she has totally lost herself. So guys your mom, sister, daughter, female cousin, aunt, grandmother, niece, fiancé or wife is not crazy and neither have you lost your mind. This is just a normal part of life and while this may not be the first time you've experienced this with her, I promise you (unless you start heading for the hills) it won't be the last. It is important therefore that you are aware that they go through this so that you will be better able to deal with and help them get through it. The Bible teaches a man to love his wife as Christ loved the church and gave himself for it (Ephesians 5:25-27). I sincerely believe that brothers towards their sisters, dads with their daughters, grandsons with the grandmothers and sons with their mothers can use this same principle, with wonderful results. It takes a willingness to sacrifice whatever is needed to make relationships work and a desire to understand and master the lessons within this book is no exception. However, as the scripture teaches we do this not only for the person, but for ourselves also. So whatever changes you need to go through or endure to build the relationship you will find that the rewards are much more than worth it. Think of it as a present to yourself.

Ephesians 5:27 continues with a discussion about Christ's relationship with the Church saying, "That he might present it unto himself a glorious church." You see it is something you are doing for them as well as you. It is a present of a relationship that is not only fulfilling, but also one that feeds you. Again, I must remind you that this will happen over and over again in the relationship, so plan on taking the time to learn what to do. Later we will be discussing how to properly respond and what steps to take to help give her back to herself so keep reading because responding to this properly has amazing benefits.

STATION IN LIFE DOES NOT MATTER

The "Eve Factor" does not discriminate. It doesn't care if a woman is married, single, wealthy, poor, underweight or overweight. It is an equal opportunity experience. We have seen ladies from all walks of life go through this experience. Most people look at the so called privileged as not having to experience certain difficulties in life, but this is not so with the "EVE FACTOR." There are those dressed in immaculately tailored clothes, freshly styled hair, expertly manicured nails, beautiful skin, driving expensive cars, wearing classy jewelry and living in fabulous homes that are totally lost. That's right in spite of all the trappings of success they cannot avoid the "EVE FACTOR." These are what I call "Glamour Girls Lost." It is an experience almost all women can relate to. If they haven't experienced it yet, all they need to do is keep living.

Glamour Girl Lost (GGL)

I suppose many of you want to know what a GGL really is, so I'll take the time to give a short description. She's fly, gorgeous, acts and talks as if she's got it all together, but when it comes to the male in her life it is all out of control. She can talk all of the talk she wants, but get her around that male in her life and you'd think that she had multiple personalities. All fun aside the GGL is sometimes hard to spot and also hard to help. They are wonderful people who have simply lost themselves and in need of a turn around.

<u>Beverly:</u> Beverly, a very successful adverting executive with her own agency touting several major accounts with *Fortune* 500 companies. She travels coast to coast on business, owns homes in three states with a penthouse apartment in Manhattan's Upper East Side, and has been in a seven-year relationship with a very successful corporate lawyer who has established his own firm consisting of a roster of 25 lawyers.

<u>Her Problem:</u> While able to purchase everything she could ever want and being everything she thought a man could desire she doesn't understand why he doesn't want to marry her. She's done everything she thought would make him love her enough to make her his wife, but after all this time (seven years) he hasn't once made the proposal. Yet she continues to give him every hint in the book. She doesn't know what she's done wrong or what's wrong with her. Maybe the only thing she's done wrong is allow herself to be strung along, totally available for his every desire and left dangling. She deserves better than that. She's a GGL.

<u>Yolanda:</u> The most popular girl in high school, most likely to succeed young woman in college and an entrepreneur to boot; Yolanda has never had a problem finding a man. However the males she chooses seem to all be losers and Charles is no exception to the rule. Initially he appeared to be a hard worker and quite motivated, but shortly thereafter he had a streak of so-called bad luck. He was going to get it together, but it was going to take a little time. He needed to stay with her for only a little while and for her to help him out while trying to get back on his feet. She agreed and he moved in, took care of things around her home, kept the place looking nice, had meals waiting for her when she got home and even rubbed her poor tired feet. She eventually exhausted herself trying to help him find a way to get back on his feet. Somehow the opportunities she made for him always sort of didn't work out and neither was the arrangement because he slowly began forgetting to do all of the wonderful things he did when he first moved in.

<u>Her Problem:</u> After sacrificing everything for his career to help him become successful; she is determined to be with a male who is stuck on the dozens. He dozen want to work, dozen want to get married, dozen want her to stop taking care of him, dozen want to sacrifice for her, dozen want her to be with other people who keep reminding her that she's being used etc. This is a GGL

<u>Corinne:</u> Like many self-assured young women in corporate America, Corinne had a definite sense of direction. She had just made Director and was definitely on her way to becoming a SVP, but her involvement with her married lover seemed to be taking its toll.

<u>Her Problem:</u> After being in a relationship with her married lover for over 10 years, having her tubes tied for him and

receiving an engagement ring she is now losing sight on her goals and coming up short with her concern for her own future while continuing to believe that he is going to leave his wife. By the way the wife is once again pregnant so he can't leave just yet. She's a GGL.

Ayanna: This lovely young woman is a very successful Real Estate investor, who has accumulated a portfolio of over fifty rental properties and an apartment building with thirty units. What is her story? Well Ayanna is yet involved with her first love that she has been dating since High-School. They have maintained an on and off again relationship for fifteen years. On the surface she looks strong and successful, but when you take a look within you'll find there's something else going on.

Her Problem: After waiting for him to finish sowing his wild oats for over fifteen years and running back to her with the promise of faithfulness and marriage, she finds herself again kicked to the proverbial curb in his life while still believing that he going to eventually come to his senses, marry her and live happily ever after. Our poor sister doesn't believe that she deserves better and is worth so much more. She needs to be honest with herself and realize you that she is the one that needs to come to their senses. She's a GGL.

Robin: This young woman has developed a successful entertainment career first as a model, then as a singer actor and now writer. She is also involved with a male that is a shrewd businessman who has pushed aside all of his ventures to manage her career. It didn't start out that way, but as she became more successful he wanted more of her time and convinced her that if he took charge of her career that he would take care of her and consequently they would have more time to be together.

Her Problem: Although the man has taken control of everything she has earned, doesn't allow her to have any decision or opinion on anything involving her finances, treats her like a piece of property and has alienated her from all those she loves she is convinced that everything is just fine and will be alright. Is this a GGL or what?

Toni: A beautiful, highly educated, cultured, excellent singer, musician and pastor's wife. Toni worked diligently with her husband in his ministry through organizing, developing and training members in the different ministries of the church while at the same time making sure that the house was a home for him and the children. Despite not being recognized or acknowledged, by her husband for the work she is doing, enduring the pressures other women bring to the table (trying to make her feel that she's not important, is in their way, flirting with her husband, constantly trying to correct her children, attempting to take her place) she continues her building process until she successfully helps the church grow to great success and consequently works herself out of a job. When you see her she appears to have it all together with all the trappings of success. The children look well groomed and cared for. She is so poised and manicured, dressed in the finest clothing, jewelry and looks the picture of success.

Her Problem: In spite of being successful at helping her husband build the ministry to the point where it is totally self-sufficient, she has no idea where she fits in, what her purpose is, or if anyone, especially her husband, knows or even cares about what she's contributed. She may look the picture of a successful pastor's wife, but mother needs replenishment. She's a GGL.

Sister Girl Lost (SGL)

<u>Joan:</u> As a youth, Joan had a responsibility to help raise her siblings but as an adult she's been unable to relinquish the reigns of responsibility. Consequently every time she seemed to be getting ahead one of her brothers had a need. She helped put one of them through college and then helped the other develop his lawn service and finally she assisted the oldest brother with his publishing business. By the way the youngest just graduated from college and is looking to Joan for help. What does Joan do? You guessed it, instead of sending him to one of the other brothers she is once again helping out. Why doesn't she take time for Joan? Sister girl is lost.

<u>Erin:</u> A wonderful young woman with two children from two different males who promised to be her everything but decided to do nothing after she became pregnant with their children. She is, at the point, where the two children are both up and walking and wouldn't you know it; along comes another Mr. Everything. They meet, she falls madly in love with him, all but neglects the two little children, becomes pregnant again while he bolts out of her life faster than lightning. Could it be that Sister Girl was lost before she met him?

Daughter Girl Lost (DGL)

<u>Sylvia:</u> An attractive young woman in her mid twenties who is somewhat estranged from her family due to being placed in a position where she was the primary caretaker for everyone in the family. You see her mom died and her dad was busy trying to make a living to support the family. She practically raised her siblings did all of the cooking,

organized and did most of the cleaning including the clothes, shopping and helped siblings with their homework. She did all of this while only a young teenager. Of course the relatives praised her for helping her dad and for being such a responsible young lady. Eventually her siblings were old enough to help her with some of the chores and take care of some things for themselves but by that time Sylvia had been doing this so long and praised so much for being a mom (and practically a wife to her dad) that she fell into the trap of feeling overly obligated.

Everyone else's needs slowly became a priority while any and everything that she needed to do for herself in due course became unimportant. Unfortunately, Sylvia started being a bit grumpy and her temperament not as cheery as it used to be. Time had passed and her father was able to accomplish great things for the family, but the demands and guilt continued; only this time in different ways. There was always something else she found herself responsible for and since she was convinced that her sense of self was wrapped up in them she continued to pour from an empty pitcher. Dad didn't notice that she was missing her entire life as a teen and brushed it off thinking she doesn't have much of an interest in going out with her friends for fun events. He wasn't aware of the fact that she spent the money he gave her for herself on the house and the needs of him and the rest of the family. One day he asked Sylvia where one of his ties was and she exploded. Needless to say no one understood what was wrong including Sylvia. Over a period of time she realized that everyone was constantly pouring from the pitcher of her life and she needed to take hold of herself and live. As sad as it may be it took her leaving the surroundings of those she loved and had given so much of herself to so that she could find herself and maintain a healthy relationship with Sylvia.

Mother/Wife Girl Lost (MGL/WGL)

<u>Pamela:</u> Pam has always been a very busy and creative person, but now her only son was graduating from high school and they needed to concentrate on his needs. Her husband took a second job to make sure that the financial side was taken care of which left Pam with handling most of the details. To make a long story short they were all successful in getting him through the school year, graduation and enrolled into college, but several months after it was all over Pam had no idea where she now belonged. She didn't know what to do with herself or how she fit into the family. This same woman, a year ago was totally vibrant, busy with her own personal projects and running a small home based business. What is wrong with her? She has lost herself by doing what she felt she had to do. In her mind no one else was going to get it done so she had to make sure it was done right. Isn't it amazing that someone that active could get to a point where she didn't know what to do with herself? What is more interesting with this wife and mom is that she didn't realize that she had lost herself.

<u>Nadine:</u> When Nadine's husband died leaving her to rear two little boys; she pulled herself together, dusted off that degree in business and went to work. She did so well at her job that she became the head of her division with a window office and all of the perks. Fortunately she was able to maintain the home by hiring someone to come in and take care of the housework, but was determined to do the cooking and have ample time for her boys. She was a great mom taking them on wonderful vacations and making sure that they had the best life had to offer she believed that they would one day become responsible young men. Despite the fact that she was able to pick up the pieces after losing her

husband and putting her boys through college and graduate school, the boys have not shown her any appreciation, but have found comfort in living back at home and enjoying the fruits of her labor. Believe it or not she is yet trying to be mama to grown men. Instead of causing them to be responsible for themselves and going on with her own life, she is now enabling them and convincing herself that she is just being a supportive mom by constantly making excuses for them. Why is she yet sacrificing so much of her life to make them comfortable? She may look like a successful businesswoman and great mother, but believe me she's a "Mother Girl Lost." Mother instead of giving a pat on the back to each son; try a kick in the rear.

Before closing out this chapter, I have one more thing to address. I know that there are those who are wondering why these women could not just pick themselves up since many of them were so active and creative prior to being lost. Well what I want to explain is that when a woman gives her all there is absolutely nothing left. Her tank is empty and the car can't go anywhere. If you turned the key the engine will not turn over. It doesn't matter how vibrant she may have been prior to losing herself, when she finally loses herself there is no air in the balloon. Consequently there is nothing for her to reach for that gives her the wherewithal to go on to anything else except replenishment. Don't forget that many of them do not even realize that they are lost. This is why we all need to become familiar with and aware of the signs so that we will know what to do to start the process of giving her back to herself.

Get The Conversation Started

Take time to discuss this with others. It can be all male or female, but may result in the most benefit when discussed among with a mixed group.

1. The "Eve Factor" deals with how women tend to lose themselves in their relationships
2. What does it actually means for her to lose herself?
3. Is it really true that the female doesn't always recognize when she is lost?
4. Most males aren't aware that females lose themselves
5. There are definite signs that can alert us as to whether she is in this state
6. This is not a one time process, but one that happens over and over again.
7. The "Eve Factor" affects females of different ages and every social-economic status.

CHAPTER TWO

THE GOOD, THE BAD & THE UGLY

There's a famous saying, "too much of a good thing can be bad." I've also heard it said that you've got to know when to say it's enough. In studying the "Eve Factor" it becomes increasingly clear that the "Eve Factor" is something that has several sides and extremes to it. On the one hand, it can be the most wonderful thing when the male understands what takes place and knows how to properly respond to it. In addition to this, though unfortunate, it can also be used and abused with dire circumstances. A woman who becomes better acquainted with the information found in this book will have the ability to better recognize when she is lost and know how to, more quickly, bring herself back to the beautiful creature God intended. Not knowing can allow her to be confused, abused and even worse allow her to sink to the point of feeling totally worthless and suicidal.

THE GOOD

In every relationship there are ups and downs that create opportunities for the relationship to stretch and grow. They are there for that very purpose. We often think that they come to wreck the relationship, but if we take the time to examine them we will realize that they are simply presenting opportunities for us to get to know each other better. We have come to the knowledge that we are different from one another. Given this understanding alone we should be persuaded to have patience with one another. Taking the time to accept the person as they are allows them as well as us room and time to grow and know. Grow from the standpoint that we recognize and learn to accept that they aren't as perfect as we thought while also finding out that we aren't either. We also gain knowledge that as we mature we learn how to better love the individual not the image. Through this process we also gain knowledge of how to better accept and love ourselves first.

The scriptures teach in I Peter 3:7 that men ought to "dwell with them according to knowledge..." What knowledge you may again ask? It is the knowledge of what it takes to love and dwell with that particular individual. It is important to understand that we have certain things that are unique to each of us and it takes time to understand them. One person may have grown up in a well-adjusted household with both parents; another may have grown up with no parents, while still another's background could be filled with great wealth. It is the through our backgrounds that our lives are shaped and it would do us a great deal of good to become familiar with where we each have come from so that we can better understand and accept one another.

The "Eve Factor" brings great opportunity for renewing relationships and building depth within a relationship. When a male understands the "Eve Factor" and properly responds to it he opens up the door for an experience that is probably never felt within the majority of relationships. It is one that is physical and deeply spiritual bringing an expression of love which saturates the mind, body and soul. It invites a love that that excuses faults and fosters openness. As the Bibles says, love covers all sins (Proverbs 10:12). The type of relationship it creates permits both male and females to be themselves without fear and creates an atmosphere where security can grow. For through its richness it enraptures one of the deepest needs that a female has. She longs and needs to be loved and cared for. The male who learns to meet this need will engender for himself great loyalty and much kindness from the females he is involved with. This is what will allow the friendships and trust to grow regardless of the type of relationship. If it is a female relative the "Eve Factor" can present a strong bonding, great sense of familial closeness, appreciation, love that reaches beyond mere words, create cherished memories and a feeling of personal wholeness in both parties. The sense of belonging that we all have a need for in our many relationships will certainly have great seeds and roots in this one. If the relationship is a romantic one, the "Eve Factor" opens, in addition to all we have previously mentioned, the opportunity to fall in love over and over again. The old feelings of infatuation that we thought were lost forever are able to spring back to life with the freshness of "puppy love" when the "Eve Factor" is properly handled. Oh yes the thrill will no longer be gone. Have you ever seen an old couple that continues to maintain the art of holding hands and being affectionate? That's the good. Have you ever seen a brother and sister reach middle age and are yet crazy about each other as well as being totally connected and supportive? That's the good. What about a dad and his grown daughter in a loving relationship with respect and mutual admiration? That's the good. Ever see a teenage young man sending his grandma a card just because? That's the good. How about a nephew coming home on his vacation to visit the aunt that raised him just to take her to see her favorite play at the theatre? That's the good. They've all stood the test of time by going through the difficulties and learning what it takes to bless one another while nurturing a relationship that feeds them both. When they both recognize the "Eve Factor" and learn what is needed to take proper advantage of the opportunity it brings to the relationship, there is nothing that can result from it but goodness.

THE BAD

The Danger of the Eve Factor
While it is wonderful to recognize the wonder of what can be achieved when we learn what to do with "The Eve Factor", the reality of what most of us face is far from being ideal. This is why we need to gain the information and become protective of our relationships because as our newspapers and news programs remind us on a daily basis it can become very dangerous. In other words, while this brings the possibilities of good things, it also holds the danger of developing into the extreme of the opposite direction. The following is a simple list of things that "The Eve Factor" can also be credited with:

a) Loss of self esteem (you end of doing so much for others that you stop taking care of you and as a consequence you may go so low that you end up doing things that will be degrading)
b) Depression
c) The possibility of suicide
d) The possibility of infidelity
e) Weight gain, food and other addictions
f) She may position herself for abuse physical/mental (when you don't love you, you also may also make it hard for others to love you)

Depression & Health

In the course of a woman losing herself there will ultimately be a bout with depression. This condition of depression has been the cause, according to physicians and chiropractors, of many health issues as well as a leading cause for suicidal tendencies. This is why it is so important to know when she has lost herself. It is so important to make sure that she takes time for self, get the proper rest and go through the process of replenishment.

I Deserve

There is an interesting thread that I've found that has been woven throughout the quilt of women who have lost themselves. It is one that if removed will allow them to separate into the beautiful individuals that they are; appreciating their lives and all that they have been blessed with. For being entangled in this tapestry, though it may be interesting to look upon, is in fact a spider's web with a tarantula waiting to eat away at the very life it has so cunningly trapped. This thread is the inability to say that I DESERVE GOOD THINGS. Oh you may not hear them say this outright, but try and give them a compliment or try to get them to do or say something good about themselves and you will be astonished.

I find that women who have lost themselves for weeks, months and even years seem to have a difficult time believing that they deserve anything good. I say this of course in reference to whatever situation that may have contributed to them being lost. In some cases they have taken the opposite point of view and actually believe they deserve everything wrong that has happened to them. Can you believe that there are women who actually believe that? Of course they do. Financial reasons are not the only reasons that the abused woman will stay in the relationship. Why do you think a woman will stay with a man who openly cheats on her or abuses her? Why is it that she would baby sit the child he bore with his mistress while they go out on a date? Why would women buy a man's love with clothes, jewelry, automobiles and expensive trips knowing that he is using her car and money to date other women? Why would a mom hang on so desperately to her son, who is doing absolutely nothing, is disrespectful and going nowhere? It could not possibly be solely predicated on her love for him. The only thing love has to do with it is that it is lacking for self. When we learn to love ourselves first, it is then that we know the limitations of how to love others. Let's take a look at Tina and Tiara. Tina and Tiara had given so much of themselves to the males in their lives that by the time I met them they had been through several relationships all of which had left them so empty that there was nothing left for them. During the course of counseling with them it became quite clear that they had lost the intrinsic value of themselves. In an attempt to bring them back to valuing themselves, I gave them assignments, one of which was to make a list of the wonderful qualities they possessed. They both found it difficult and almost impossible to do. I told Tina to go and buy some bath products and take some special time to pamper herself. I gave Tiara a similar task and to my surprise they both in different sessions told me that it was a waste of time and I replied that it was not a waste of time because they were worth spending that little extra time on. When I asked them if they felt the same way about themselves, to my utter shock they replied with a look and words that said that they were not worth it. Not worth taking to extra time to pamper yourself with a simple bath. Stop reading and think about that for a moment. If this describes you or someone you know, please understand that this is a dangerous place to be. It is time for a reality check. You cannot properly love someone else without first loving yourself. If you are not getting the love you desire it is because you are not first giving it to yourself! In fact the love that you are giving to someone else is not necessarily love at all. It may be an attempt to hold on to something that doesn't exist. Think about it! If you are constantly being hurt by the person you are trying to hold on to regardless if it is intentional, known or unknown on their part (sometimes they are not hurting you at all it is simply an unrealistic expectation on your part that they are not meeting), then you need to reevaluate what you are looking for. First and foremost you need to begin to give yourself the love and time you deserve. By the way, YOU DO DESERVE WHAT'S GOOD. You are worth much more than you realize. Take a little extra time with yourself. You cannot start from anywhere else. You must start with you. You are God's highest creation in the earth! He saved the best for last! He didn't leave you on the ground after creation, so why are you still there? You are a woman not a rug!

I had to start Tiara's list for her naming all of the wonderful things that she had done. I mixed them up and put them into a story. I told her about a female friend of mine who; edifying her as I went along. I told her that I wanted her to help me help this friend. After finishing up the story I then asked her what she thought of the woman. She went on to tell me what an incredible person my friend was and how much she admired her. Of course she was shocked to find I was not talking about someone else at all, but that she was indeed that woman. Just like Tina and Tiara, there are too many women out there who need to change their self-image through the use of proper language. Some call it "self-talk." Whatever you want to call it, you must find a way to talk to yourself about yourself in a better light.

The scriptures teach, "As a man thinketh in his heart so is he." Sister you need to realize that life beats you up enough as it is, you don't need to give it any assistance. This is a battle that you can win! Don't look at it as an abnormal experience, but as one that comes to give us a little time to replenish and re-focus on self through a reevaluation of where you are at this point in your lives. Understand that you react or respond based on what has been programmed into your computer (read: your brain).

Our brain was created in such a way that we are able to program it through our five senses. This programming results in our actions and reactions. If you were embarrassed because you attempted to step out and try something new, then chances are the next time you attempt to try something new your brain will bring up that memory. It's a great thing the brain does because it also protects us from danger and harm. If you've stepped off a curb and had to quickly jump back on the sidewalk to avoid getting hit by a truck, the next time you'll first look both ways before leaving the curb. These experiences create the memories and the voices in our heads that we hear when we need to make decisions etc. It is these same voices in our head that talk to us allowing us to reason and act. These same voices may also cripple us if our minds have been fed too much negative information. As I said earlier we program our brains. How? Through our senses, however, we are especially susceptible to words.

The saying "sticks and stones will break my bones, but words will never hurt me" is a lie. More people have been permanently scarred by words while the wounds and breaks from all the sticks and stones have long since healed. Think about good and bad news. If you get bad news from a doctor, before ever getting a second opinion you start feeling worse. When someone tells you that you've inherited millions of dollars from a relative you've never met, your sickness instantly disappears, you begin to walk in spite of the fact that your legs don't work and the only blue you recognize is the newly found bright sky that you will be enjoying from the cruise ship you'll soon be on. For this same reason you are also affected by words that you personally speak to yourself. Actually you sort of hear those words twice. What do I mean? Well, have you ever heard your voice on a tape recorder? It doesn't actually sound like you does it? That is because you are accustomed to hearing it from both your inner ear and outer ear. When you hear it on a tape recording you are only hearing it from your outer ear. Therefore, when you talk negative talk to yourself it is like hearing it twice. Not only that, you normally say negative things with emotion allowing it to move into the subconscious mind more readily. Unfortunately you cannot erase this, but on the other hand you can dilute it and add some new and improved information in. The combination of negative self-talk, giving so much of yourself to others and the lack of replenishment can easily bring you to the point of feeling that you do not deserve good things. Do yourself a favor and try this. Listen to the thoughts that go through your mind and examine them. You will find that if you are going to make any change in your life it will have to start with the changing of these conversations. As you identify what you say to yourself, you can then begin saying, with emotion, the things that are more positive about yourself. It is these things that will help you to come to the place where you can actually believe again that YOU DESERVE GOOD THINGS. In fact say it now. I DESERVE GOOD THINGS! I DESERVE TO BE HAPPY! I AM A WONDERFUL PERSON! GOD CREATED ME TO HAVE LIFE AND THAT MORE ABUNDTANTLY! Now go ahead and start throwing some long needed love on yourself because YOU DESERVE!

THE UGLY

A female is extremely vulnerable when she's lost and it is at this time that so many of them have been taken advantaged of. In other words, it is when things begin to get ugly. It is at this point where we begin to see the doors slowly opening for abuse, misuse and, at its worst death. While the males carry much of this out in the relationship, some of these negative actions towards the female don't always come from external sources. Sometimes the female remains in her situation much too long and end up destroying herself. Of course this is not a book of blame, but one that intends to give tools to make your relationships better. So lets move forward in exploring the dark side of the "Eve Factor."

Infidelity

When a married woman loses herself the husband also loses her, but doesn't realize it. Not only is she vulnerable, he too is quite vulnerable and is a target for infidelity. Now don't get me wrong; the woman losing herself is not a reason or excuse for anyone to be unfaithful, but if it is not attended to, it can set the stage for the idea to come in and take root. What in the world are you talking about? I'm glad you asked. When a woman becomes lost, regardless how physically beautiful she is, she becomes less attractive to the male. It doesn't necessarily mean that she physically looks any different or has, as is sometimes the case, stopped taking special time to properly groom herself. It is just that the part of her that she loses is that which gives a woman "The Fragrance" (see chapter on What Makes A Woman Beautiful') or what truly makes a male attracted to her. Let's take a look at Dr. Derrick Steiner and his wife Sherry:

Dr. Derrick & Sherry Steiner:

While Dr. Steiner was a medical student his wife Sherry worked and supported him. They had many things they wanted to accomplish and top priority was helping Derrick get through medical school. Through the years it was tough on both of them especially when Derrick was going through his internship. At that point they had two beautiful little children, a girl and a boy, and didn't see as much of each other due to their hectic schedules. Her working to support the family, handling house chores and two little children ages two and five. He was trying to get through his residency and help Sherry with the children and house as often as he could. As time went on Sherry began to lose herself. Gone was the beautiful curvaceous figure, immaculately styled hair, professionally manicured nails and arched eyebrows. There was a time he thought that she looked beautiful with her hair a little messy. However now, it seemed that she was a bit more in need of his time than she usually was and she acted somewhat strangely confused. He didn't mind her needing him, but wasn't used to her being that needy and clingy. She was no longer the strong supporting person that he was used to and when he tried to talk to her to find out what was wrong, try as she might, she couldn't tell him. When he tried as hard as he could to help her and solve the problem, he wasn't able to understand that she didn't want him to solve anything; she simply wanted him to listen. He wasn't used to that, especially since the plan had been working so well the last few years and they were so close to him finishing his residency. Because he was not aware of the "Eve Factor" or how to properly handle that type of situation he became frustrated. And as usual there is someone who is able to understand his frustration; Suzy Jane.

The funny thing about Suzy is that she has incredible similarities to Sherry. She doesn't necessarily look like her, but she certainly wears her hair like Sherry used too. Hey, wait a minute. She sort of dresses the way Sherry used to and even has some of the same little traits like her too, like her laugh and the way she sort of holds her mouth when she's contemplating on what she is about to say. Do you understand what's going on? In many cases when a wife loses herself the husband goes looking for her in someone else. That's why ladies the other woman often has some of your characteristics. Now please understand I have observed this in situations where the woman has lost herself and it resulted in an infidelity. Again, I must reiterate that a woman losing herself is not a reason or excuse for a man being unfaithful.

Now here's the peculiar part. Derrick eventually graduates, he and Sherry get a divorce and two years later Sherry finds herself again. She gets in shape, begins to truly love herself, starts her own business and somehow ends up at the same event as Dr. Derrick and Suzy Jane. As Sherry steps into the room, looking as wonderful as the day that Derrick first set his eyes on her with the knowledge that she didn't need him, but he certainly needed her, the "Fragrance" of her femininity was flowing all over that room! Derrick, standing there with Suzy Jane on his arm, was completely taken in by her beauty. It wasn't just the clothes, makeup or hair, but that something special that was originally manufactured by Sherry. His mouth was opened so wide that you could moisten envelops on his tongue and he wouldn't realize what took place. He was so caught up with staring at Sherry that he forgot he had Suzy on his arm. Realizing that Derrick wasn't responding to her conversation Suzy noticed that he was staring at some other woman and to her amazement it was his ex-wife Sherry. She smacked him in the head and said "don't you see me standing here?" However, he didn't understand a word she had said. Now why do you suppose he was more attracted to his ex-wife and totally oblivious to the young woman he left her for? By the way from that point on he was steadily pursuing Sherry. It is somewhat complicated, but the main reason is that Sherry is the real thing and Suzy Jane is the imitation Sherry. You see when Sherry found herself again she became the person that Derrick originally fell in love with. Is that crazy or what? Regardless of how crazy this scenario may appear, the truth is we all see it happening every single day and have probably been victims of it ourselves. Due to not being aware of the "Eve Factor" many have destroyed their marriages, children, themselves and their future.

Abuse
Unfortunately there are some very disturbed people in our world. One of the saddest things about them is that they are able to hide in the most unsuspecting places. They are people with the most respectable titles and are able to live what we would call a double life. Sometimes they have been abused themselves and don't understand what love truly is. Tragically they are people who do not love themselves and end up using control to make someone else stay with them. Such is the case of Joseph and Ophelia Thomas.

Joseph and Ophelia Thomas
Joseph was a minister in a Pentecostal church and was widely respected. Ophelia was also reared Pentecostal in a wonderful home with parents who loved one another. Unfortunately in Joseph's home there was much violence where his father ruled with an iron fist. While he was an alcoholic spending most of his pay on gambling and carousing, his mother worked hard to keep food on the

table and take care of the family. Many a night his Dad would come in tearing through the house, fighting his mother and beating him and his sisters out of pure frustration derived from his own guilt ridden affairs, failures as a man or money he had lost in a card game. This was a pattern that would be deeply engrained within the consciousness of young Joseph, but didn't seem to rise to the surface until after he and Ophelia were married and she had given so much of herself to him and the family that she began to lose herself.

Instead of knowing how to properly communicate with his young wife, Joseph began to be abusive. No in the beginning he didn't hit her at all (but you must understand if a man is calling a woman every vile thing that he can think of hitting her is just around the corner). And when a woman is lost, she is in a very vulnerable situation. She already feels bad about herself. All she needs to sink to her lowest low is someone who seemingly instinctively knows how to bring her to the bottom. Unfortunately, Joseph had been educated in this first hand. Of course no one at church was aware of what was going on but as you can imagine things began to slip out.

Slowly Joseph began to cause her to alienate herself from everyone who was ever close to her. The family began to notice that she wouldn't come over or call like she used to. Her best friend, Joyce, couldn't understand why she stopped speaking to her and why this distant, totally insecure person who couldn't think for herself replaced her normal jovial outgoing self. The fear of her leaving was too much of a risk, so subconsciously he would make her stay through alienation and intimidation. It stopped being love and now became possession.

I realize most people don't want to see it that way, but if the road sign is saying that you are heading in that direction (and it is), then you've got to open your eyes and stop lying to yourself. Not only do you need to stop lying, you also have to admit to yourself what is actually happening. It is always difficult to admit to yourself things that seem to be so unreal or embarrassing. We often say to ourselves "this couldn't possibly be true. This couldn't possibly be happening." In this case Ophelia was saying some of the same things. She felt guilty and embarrassed for being in this situation and for allowing the fairytale vision of what marriage was suppose to be, sink into what had now become a nightmare. She was too ashamed to share all that was going on in her household and when she did begin to share, it only served to cause her to sink deeper into the abyss that was now what seemed to be her destiny. The ministers she confided in simply told her to be a more loving and considerate wife and that she should stick with him. When she did talk to loved ones they became caught up with the idea of helping her stay in the marriage and the embarrassment it would cause the ministry. This they did not to harm her, but to help them stay together. Unfortunately, there seems to be no true marriage counseling for the minister who had serious issues in his life whether it is marriage, personal, financial or family because the minister is simply supposed to have it together. How sad. The abuse had eventually become physical; the signs were quite obvious and got to the point where she was wearing sunglasses as a cover her bruises. There were even times when she was not allowed to come to church and sometimes couldn't due to the physical abuse. To make matters worse, Joseph began having an affair using the justification of the other woman being more supportive and spiritually in tune with his ministry. Her friends and family members were aware of most of what was going on, but because of religious traditions some their beliefs about divorce and separation prevented them from helping her come from under her situation. It wasn't that they didn't love her, but they were all stuck in the misleading trap of tradition. They thought that a woman had to stay with someone regardless of how they were being treated. This may sound insane to you, but they thought that by doing this they were keeping her soul from being lost, from going to hell and saving her family. There she was caught between doing what she felt was right and the literal possibility of losing her life. This woman was being trapped by what she thought was God's will, disappointing family and surviving. Please understand that I do not advocate divorce. What I do advocate is separation and survival (I Corinthians 7:10-16). (How did this situation end? It could have ended in many ways. I want you to think about it. I'll leave it up to you to figure out how it possibly ended.)

Depression/Addiction/Suicide
For most of us addiction and suicide will never be an option, but for those that fall deep into depression there looms the demons of oppression with voices that appear to be thoughts in the mind telling them that these are viable options.

The depression can get so bad that they are unable to get out of bed for days and weeks. The confusion and emotional/spiritual pain they are experiencing is so great that the only thing they want to do is escape it at any cost. It is in times like these that the demons of addiction offer there brand of devilish alternatives. It doesn't matter what addiction you may turn to alcohol, sex, drugs or food, they all enslave you and bring you down much lower than you were prior to ever tasting their vicious nectar. They only give you a false temporary relief from your pain and before you know it you are doing things you are too ashamed to mention.

"And sin, when it is finished bringeth forth death" (James 1:25).That's right, after you have gone to your lowest low that filthy enemy of the soul SUICIDE starts talking to your mind attempting to convince you that you feel that taking your life is now the only alternative. Hold on a minute. Let's just take one step back. First of all those thoughts did not come from you nor did they come from Jesus. They came directly from the pit of HELL. God's intention is that you LIVE and not only that, but to LIVE LIFE MORE ABUNDANTLY (John 10:10)! You don't have to die nor do you have to be enslaved by your addictions because Jesus came to make you free from sin and death (Romans 8:2). Don't believe all the lies that tell you that He won't hear you. Come on right now begin to pray and ask the Lord to forgive you of your sins and clean you up from your filthiness. His word says that though your sins are like scarlet He will make you so clean that you will be whiter than snow (Isaiah 1:18). Talk to Him from the sincerity of your heart and He will hear you. Pray to Him in Jesus name and receive your deliverance. Block out those negative thoughts and press your way through to the savior. He'll bring peace and comfort to your troubled mind.

GOD'S PORTION/YOUR PORTION

Before I go any further I would like to say something to the ladies. Giving of your Self to others is a noble and wonderful thing but there are two things you must know. First of all, you must know that there is a limit at which you can give of yourself. Secondly, there is a part of you that belongs only to you and God. It doesn't belong to your friends, children, house, business, parents, anything or anyone else, but you and God! When you give that part of you away, then there is nothing remaining for you. The truth is, when you have given that part of you away everyone, including yourself, has lost you. It is time for replenishment. Do it not for anyone else, but you. Please understand that loving self is not selfish. It is self-preservation. The Bible says "save your self." Guys, it is so vital that you recognize that A FEMALE MUST BE REPLENISHED!

CHAPTER THREE

THE PURPOSE OF HER CREATION?

I have often heard motivational speaker Zig Ziglar say that "Necessity is the mother of invention and the architect of success." I am quite moved at how we are able to create things that make life much better for us. Things like the telephone, stove, eyeglasses, cars, computers, the electric light and a host of other wonderful things. Not only do these things make life easier, but they also fit the purpose for which they were created for extremely well. Of course you could use the back of a screwdriver to hammer in a nail, but wouldn't it be better used for its intended purpose? This brings us to the point that we create things to fulfill a specific purpose. So it is with the woman. She was created with a specific purpose in mind. According to the book of beginnings, Genesis, God looked at man and realized that it was not good for him to be alone and decided that He would make a help meet for him (Genesis 2:18). The perfect help that he created was the woman. In dealing with the female it is important that we understand why she was created for in knowing the purpose for her creation we are given insights that will help us better relate to her.

HELP MEET

Genesis 2:18 says, "And the Lord God said, it is not good that the man should be alone; I will make him a help *meet* for him."

Over the course of time there have been varied views of this wonderful Scripture expressed by a myriad of theologians, but I believe one of the most wonderful truths has been overlooked when it comes to the relationship of the sexes. That wonderful truth revolves around why she was created; the purpose for which she was created. The Bible says that God created a help *meet* for the man, Adam who was the only human being in existence. One of the meanings of the word alone is: without aid or support. Isn't that interesting that here was this man God created who seemingly had everything including his own planet; yet he needed help? Man had been given a job to not only take care of the garden and name animals, but to also have dominion. This supreme authority and ownership was to be specifically over all the fish in the sea, the birds in the air, everything that is on the earth and including the earth itself. In order to accomplish this task he needed assistance but not just any assistance. God felt he needed one that was perfectly suitable for him, support that was just right. That's why he took a bone from Adam's body and created Eve. Again, please keep in mind that he did not need just any old help, but help that was **meet** for him. Did you notice how I phrased that sentence? He didn't say helpmate, but help *meet*. Let's break down the meaning of these words.

Help means to assist or give aid, meet means just right, perfectly suitable or perfectly fitting. Therefore God was creating an assistant that was perfectly suitable or just right for the man. Well you may say, "that's nice, but what does that have to do with anything?" It has everything to do with the relationship between males and females and is not limited to those that involve romantic love. Most importantly it tells us why and for what she was created.

She was created as the perfect assistant to the man helping him to have success in whatever endeavor he ventures into. For this reason she naturally gives herself to him. I'm not talking about sexual relationships. Rather about how a woman, intrinsically, pours so much of herself into where a man is going in life and helps him achieve. She inherently gravitates to assisting the males in her life accomplish, grow and progress. She's always attempting to help him improve, see more than one side to a situation, believe that he can be more than he currently is, go after more than he has etc. No one has to tell her to do this because she instinctively gives of herself to his development, growth and success. That's right, she was created not only to be the perfect assistant (help meet) but also to also help him subdue, have dominion and to ultimately rule with him over whatever it is they both achieve.

The saying "behind every good man is a good woman" is more than a nice proclamation; it is a statement of truth. The female is one of the most wonderful gifts that God has given to the male. As Apostle Paul states, "Neither was the man created for the woman; but the woman for the man" (I Corinthians 11:9). I am aware that some may not agree with what is being revealed here, but regardless of your belief in the Bible or God, you cannot deny the fact that a female instinctively gives of herself to the males in her life. She does what she was created to do. She helps the male grow and achieve.

WHO MOVED THE "HELP WANTED" SIGN?

Almost every summer whether, I stayed in New York City or visited with relatives in the south, I looked for some type of employment. In my endeavor to seek employment there was always one indicator that opportunity was abound, the good old "Help Wanted" sign. Usually you would go in and inquire about the job and when you were hired they removed the sign indicating that help was either no longer needed or wanted. Sometimes there were no "Help Wanted" signs at all and I had to be quite clever in helping the establishment realize that they actually needed assistance but didn't realize it at that time. The most interesting scenario I encountered, however, was when there, was a sign in the window but the store owners were not even aware it was there. Regardless of the situation, my position was that I was there to help.

This last scenario is describes the type of male who are walks around with this "Help Wanted" sign on his foreheads with absolutely no knowledge that it exists. In many cases, he doesn't know he needs help, he's too proud to ask for help and at worst doesn't want to be helped. On the other hand, you have the female who is naturally inclined to the business of investing in males who sometimes have no idea what she is doing or why she is doing it. Unfortunately, this lack of understanding, on the part of some males, has caused them to sometimes view her as the enemy. I want to inform all males that she is not the enemy but is there for your good.

The Bible declares "She will do him good and not evil all the days of her life" (Proverbs 31:12). Not only was she created for this very purpose; she's extremely good at it. So let us begin to change our view of her as our enemy to now seeing her as our closest friend and ally. Females, however, need to understand that their gift is to help and not to change.

Attempting to change the male brings frustration, but helping him brings success and happiness. Unfortunately, every male is not willing to receive help. I implore females to avoid this type of male like the plague! She is much better off investing her time in other things because this type of involvement can cause her much harm and results in time and talent being totally wasted. People that need help and don't want it are like a parked car that thinks it is on its way somewhere. It is futile in her thinking that she is going to help anyone who's a parked car. They are males with extraordinary talent, potential and talk dripping off of them, but are doing absolutely nothing with it. They are keenly aware of their abilities, but only use them as a spider's web to lure in an unsuspecting female into believing that they are eventually going to do something. My advice to the female is simply this: run! Nevertheless females have the innate desire and ability to help males achieve success. To this end the woman was created with some very special qualities that enable her to be effective in her purpose. She has what we like to call the "EVABILITIES."

THE "EVABILITIES"

"Faster than a speeding bullet, more powerful than a locomotive, able to leap tall buildings in a single bound." Those are the words that not only show Superman's differences from the ordinary man, but also show why he is able to be man's hero in the make believe city of Metropolis. When we look at the female's creation we also see that she, too, has been given special abilities that enable her to fulfill her role as the perfectly suitable assistant to the male.

I know that there is someone out there thinking that I am saying that the only thing a female is good for and limited to be is assisting, working with and supporting the male. That is not at all what I am saying, however I am saying that she was created for that purpose and is specifically gifted in that area. She has been given the gift of being able to see what he doesn't, hear what he does not, know what he does not know and to top it all off she has the "Gift of Influence." One might wonder why these? Well if she couldn't see, hear and know what the male in her life doesn't and has no influence with him, then how could she possibly help him? These abilities are given and enhanced by her ability to use both sides of the brain. The logical and creative sides are played out in what we call the EVABILITIES.

Seeing The Unseen

In her innate desire to have a meaningful relationship with a male, whether it is her brother, son, father or cousin, a female is naturally protective of it and every positive thing that results from it. Consequently, she is able to see his blind spots. I've seen females warn their unsuspecting males about shady business partners, so-called friends that are using him, females that want more than a platonic relationship and the holes he doesn't see in his get rich quick scheme. Enhanced by the tendency to think from a right-brain perspective, she is able to give broader view of a given situation. While the male is focusing on a given detail, she is looking at the entire picture. For example he may be focusing on a child's rebellion, while she may also see that the child is crying out for attention and is not merely being disobedient or unruly. So there is a need to address the entire situation as opposed to disciplining the child for the one incident. Another way of understanding the fact that males tend to focus while females are able to take in everything around them is to view it from the perspective of the driver and passenger of a car. The driver's view is limited by the necessity to focus on the road while the passenger is free to enjoy all of the totality of the scenic view.

There are three females that immediately come to mind when I think of how females are able to take in the entire picture while the male is focused on the one detail he is working on. They are my wife, Sharon, and friends, Marion Thompson and Eveleen Harrison. I have been quite fortunate to work with all three of these magnificent ladies. Of course, my wife and I have partnered on numerous projects and I have learned to appreciate her ability to see the big picture. In fact, whenever I am doing anything I love to leave the organizing to her and believe it or not take charge of the different tasks that need to be done. I don't know of anyone who can organize anything any better than Sharon. I have seen her take a children's choir from 4 members to 72, put together plays and arrange all types of trips. Initially, I thought she was being overly critical about everything I was doing but after swallowing my pride I began to realize that she was simply trying to help me out. When I finally figured that out, being the kind of person that I am, I was ready to jump right in. I was constantly running things past her. It got so bad that she was somewhat overwhelmed and felt that she didn't want to be constantly telling me what to do. (Isn't that funny?) Nevertheless, we both got over our little issues and figured out that we complemented each other's strengths and weaknesses. We have since become a great team! Some of the best times we have together are when we are brainstorming over some project or idea. I love working with my wife!

Let me reiterate, however, that it took time before we were able to understand what each other's strengths are and that we, as a team, could truly accomplish much more working together than apart. (By the way, it took nothing away from my manhood to listen to the wisdom of a female). My friend Marion is another incredible woman. We were both employed together when she became project leader. What I noticed about her was that she had a keen sense of the overall scope of this huge project from the end to the beginning. No, I didn't make a mistake, I said from the end to the beginning. She saw it like an aerial view of a maze and knew exactly how to get us where we needed to go in a cost effective, yet fun, manner. There were at least two other males working with her. Time after time, we were all amazed at how she could articulate the vision and details of the project bringing together each piece that we were individually working on. Showing us where and how our individual pieces related, she was able to allow us to use our strengths to accomplish our tasks while considering the other's needs. Realizing that handing the overall project was her strength and bathing in single pieces did more to hinder her and us; the team of males followed my lead in taking the small tasks off of her hands. Needless to say the project came in early and under budget.

Eveleen, like Marion, is also a great leader. Knowing how to gather the pieces and bring excitement to what would normally be monotonous work by her sheer joy and excitement of conquering the project. That's a quality males get excited over. We love to conquer things.

These females did not emasculate the males around them, but worked as equal team members with them encouraging their sense of manhood by soliciting their ideas, opinions and allowing them to fully take the initiative where needed. Which brings me to another point; one of the most wonderful things a female is able to see is the male's potential. She sees it long before he does. Have you ever noticed how a male may seem to have very little potential at all, who, after becoming involved with the right female, improves to the point that we don't recognize him? After his change you can hear statements like "is that Joe?", "I had no idea he was capable of so much," and "she has certainly made a difference in him!" When you think about it her investment in him is based solely on what she was able to see in him. Some of you may be saying that these are occasions when she finds a weak male, but I beg to differ. Sometimes he's one that has never thought of doing some of the things she can see him doing and as a result never pursued them; her ability to perceive is amazing. However, it must be noted that this ability is so normal to her that it sometimes becomes difficult for her to understand why he is not able to see what she does. Both parties must therefore give special attention to this insight or it can result in communication problems or worse (see "She's Not Against The Plan"). Her EVABILITY to see what he normally does not see is part of her being the perfect partner for him. Although it is different from the male's ability, it is complementary to it and if used properly can result in better decision-making, a greater partnership with her and most of all a newfound respect and appreciation for the male-female relationship.

Hearing The Unheard
Have you ever noticed that in a room full of babies where only one is crying, and the mother, although in another room, is able to distinguish between all of them and know when it is her baby? She can usually tell you why the baby is crying. I have even heard of women knowing if a dog needs water, wants to go for a walk, sees trouble or hasn't been feed based solely on the way it barks. There are times when someone will say something and the male will understand it one way but the female will hear and understand what the male perceived and also what he

didn't. It seems that she hears with more than her ears. She hears with her ears, eyes and feelings. A Female tends to take in all of those factors while listening to what is being communicated. Although it may seem she is not paying attention or not hearing what's going on, you can rest assured that when it comes to protecting what you have she is more than locked in on the action. She is sometimes like the airport scanners examining everything visible, non-visible, hearing the spoken and unspoken.

Knowing The Unknown

"You see, "First Ladies" seem to smell a rat! They pick up on unclean spirits. They detect a sister or brother with an ulterior motive! They can tell when something isn't right! They just do! It's God given insight!" (1*First Lady, Carolyn Vinson pg 22 ISBN 1-931323-00-3 © 2000)

A woman sometimes just knows things. It's not that she has seen heard or even read anything about it she just knows. We often refer to it as a "woman's intuition." However, I don't attribute this totally to right-brain thinking, but rather a spiritual awareness that I believe is within every one of us and is perhaps more pronounced in females. It is sometimes a prophetic and discerning ability that comes from God.

Have you ever heard of a mother who admonished her child to not go somewhere and when the child asks why the mom says, "Because I said so"? The reason she told the child this is was not because she knew exactly what was going to take place, but that she had a feeling that it would not be good for them to go at this time. Wouldn't you know that it turned out that if the child would have gone there was certain danger or trouble waiting? Not only have I heard that, I have actually lived it. My mom could not explain how she knew, she just did. There are countless times that females did things and didn't know why but they did it based on a feeling. Some say it was God speaking to them; others want to say it was intuition. Whatever you want to attribute it to, females seem to just know things. I encourage them to not ignore this, for many have ignored this with bad consequences.

The Gift Of Influence/Persuasion

With a simple look, smile, batting of her eyelashes or a short sentence, it is said that the most fragile woman can weaken the strongest man on earth. It is no secret that a female has the gift of influence/persuasion with males. Just look at the story of Samson and Delilah (Judges 16).

Samson was an Israelite with the presence of God on him at times that allowed him to defeat over a thousand men. When his enemies, the Philistines realized that they could do nothing to defeat him they found a woman. This woman was able to do what an entire army of men could not. She didn't use a sword or any other military weapon but armed only with her ability to influence and persuade she defeated their greatest foe.

Then there's Abigail and David (I Samuel 25). Abigail's husband offended David to the point that he was bringing over 400 experienced men of war to her home to annihilate every living person in her home. Abigail found out what her husband had done and decided to go meet David and convince him not to destroy her entire household. There David was riding at "break neck" speed, in a fit of anger and blood in his eyes heading for Abigail's home when all of a sudden he saw Abigail loaded down with the supplies that David and his men needed. She was able to stop him, compliment him and ultimately persuade him that what he was going to do was a bad idea.

Look at Henry Ford's wife. She was able to convince him that he was really going to be successful in his quest to build the "horseless carriage," the automobile, and look where that got him. Of course now if it was totally left up to her she would have thought of building it in a place where there was a door big enough to drive it out of after it was finished, but that's an entirely different story.

A hundred people can tell a man that he is nothing but a total loser and that same man can go home feeling kind of low but if the female in his life tells him that those people have absolutely no clue as to what they are talking about and proceeds to tell him what a great guy he is; believe me that man is going to believe her over the hundred. At the same time, those same people can do the same thing and he might brush it off but if the female in his life says he's no good, he will not be able to handle it. What she says weighs very heavily on him. Most successful men have had great women believing in them, she sees him as what he can be long before he does and has the ability to speak it into his life.

Have you ever heard a woman calling him what she saw he could be? It is a clearly documented fact that it was the vision of Mary Todd Lincoln that ultimately projected her husband into the presidency. Let me again say that a female has great influence with the males in her life. Look at how young boys all but break their necks doing feats to impress females. I sincerely believe that every achievement a male makes is ultimately influenced by his desire to impress some female. It doesn't matter if it is his mom, sister, wife, girlfriend or some female he is interested in; I believe that she influences every accomplishment. What in the world do you think would make Adam give up all that he owned including life itself? He didn't want to lose that woman! She was able to influence him. The serpent understood that. Why do you think he didn't approach Adam himself? Instead, he approached the one he knew Adam would respond to.

There was a time when a male couldn't get a date unless he had a job and a car. And you know what? The laziest male would go out and get himself a job, scrape and save just to get himself a car. Unfortunately today too many females have dropped their standards and have allowed males to look to them to supply those luxuries. I knew the time when a young man had to dress his best because it was a requirement of the female. In fact many-a-male, after becoming involved with a female, upgraded his appearance so drastically that most of his friends didn't recognize him. I knew a guy who always looked a bit shabby. After he started dating this young woman, he shaved, got a haircut, changed his clothes and even started shinning his shoes! People said they didn't know the old boy could look that good.

There are many females that are able to bring out the best in some males. Some who we felt were failures ended up becoming successful businessmen simply because the female believed in, encouraged and gave him the nudge he needed to move forward. It is totally amazing.

I've seen the lazy, shiftless son leave his mama's house and become extremely competent. While his mama was stunting his growth, the new woman in his life encouraged his growth. Why? She saw potential! I tell you if it were not for females we would probably be living in caves instead of nice homes and apartments. Her disapproving looks, body language and words have the ability to put literal fear of presenting his opinions and ideas to her.

Ladies, if you want the male in your life to shut down on you, open your mouth with negative words, fill your stares with disapproval and cross your arms when he wants to talk to you. Or simply, put down his opinions altogether. You see a male wants to know that the female is a safe haven for his ideas and in his corner at all times. He may be lying through his teeth in public and everyone is telling him so, but if the female in his life tells him he's lying in front of those same people; it becomes war. There are endless stories I could relate here on the power of female persuasion, but I'll just leave you with this: Ladies please remember when the male hears your words, sees your gestures and posture, that they have great influence with him. So be careful. It is a gift from God so that you may use it to bless and not abuse.

SHE IS NOT AGAINST THE PLAN

You know, it is amazing how many females are in agreement with the above statement, while just as many males disagree with it. Maybe I need to clarify the statement a little more. There is an enemy out there that does not want males and females working together and unfortunately we end of thinking that it's each other. The true enemy is communication or the lack of knowledge in that area. Let me further break it down like this: In every male there is the ability to work a plan. However, one of the things he may have serious problems with is sharing that plan with the female in his life.

In his mind, he initially thinks that she is going to applaud and congratulate him for being a man with a vision. He sees himself as doing a great thing by either coming up with this great idea or for discovering this wonderful way that can truly help them reach their goals and achieve their dreams. Surely the female in his life will have faith in him. Unfortunately, in too many cases, she ends up either laughing at the idea thinking it's a joke, shooting a million holes in it by showing him all of the problems with his "great idea" or makes statements about the idea that causes him feel lower than an ant's belly. I know that many of you guys are thinking that she's the enemy but believe it or not SHE IS NOT AGAINST THE PLAN!

Before we go further into that let us look at what happens to her in these situations. First of all, she feels that she has to help him and secondly she has to protect everything they've accomplished up to that point. Whether it is a conscience thing or not a woman feels that she has to assist the man in becoming what he needs to be and doing what he needs to do. There is that innate ability that allows her to use this wonderful skill of actually helping him find success, regardless of what he is striving for. She doesn't even have to have expertise in the field of work. Remember the EVABILITIES? She can see the good, the pitfalls and also those areas that we have not considered. It is the seeing what he cannot, hearing what he cannot and knowing what he does not that she brings to the table that gives him the edge he so desperately needs, but so often cannot recognize. The problem we are facing here, however, is a lack of understanding on both of their parts. Neither is aware that the EVABILITIES, while necessary in this situation, can be somewhat brutal to the male ego.

Let me explain. The female is extremely protective of everything that has already been accomplished by the two of them, so her sense of security automatically kicks in. Secondly, she is able to see the areas in your plan that need further investigation so clearly that she doesn't understand why you are not aware of them. Consequently, the way she states her findings to the male is often in a condescending tone. Why? It is because she thinks he either knows about the problems and is running aimlessly out there after a pipe dream while putting everything they have in jeopardy or is too caught up over the idea to realize it. Regardless to which one is true she does not want them to lose!

Is she against the plan? No. Then why does he get so bent out of shape when she points things out to him? It is because he heard it from the male's perspective. The only thing he heard was an attack on his plan and his manhood. Remember her EVABILITY of persuasion and influence? When she points out the problems with the plan in an effort to get him to handle them prior to executing what could be a great plan, he hears them in a condescending manner and is deeply affected by her words. I'll repeat that. He is deeply affected by her words.

Actually it is the presentation of those words that cut him off at the knees. Is she really trying to stop him from being progressive, proactive and fulfilling his place as a man? No, but she is not always aware of the power of her influence nor its presentation. She wants him to take the initiative, but she doesn't want him to do it blindly and recklessly that they lose everything. What am I saying? SHE IS NOT AGAINST THE PLAN. What is needed, however, is an understanding on the part of the female of how she articulates her findings as it relates to his plan. Don't kill the man!

Too many ladies lose their men to other females by simple incidents like this. His ego is destroyed and some other female, who understands how to work with a male, scoops him up and he becomes wildly successful. What a tragedy. I'm not saying allow him to walk over a cliff, but rather to learn how to properly communicate to him what he is not considering in the plan. On the other hand, males must be aware that a female will protect what you both have created to the point of fighting him if necessary. She doesn't want him to ruin everything they've worked so hard to earn. Understand that she's in protective mode and that she sees these things so clearly that she can't understand why you don't. I know it comes across as if she is calling you stupid but it is also your responsibility to help her learn to communicate with you effectively.

We don't come out of the womb knowing these things. We all have to learn. When you both understand what is going on in this situation, you'll be better able to take advantage of what you have before you. So guess what? She's not against the plan instead she is protecting your cake so that it will be there after you've also acquired the milk.

THE VIRTUOUS WOMAAN (Proverbs 31)

In the 31st chapter of the book of Proverbs, we find a description of what has been viewed as the ultimate woman. Men read this chapter in the Bible and imagine themselves having a woman like this and women view it as something to aspire to, but sometimes see it as unachievable. This woman described is neither man's concoction nor the general image suggested by most women. What it is may surprise most people who have heard this chapter taught or preached. They are requirements/qualities given to King Lemeuel by his mother for the type of woman he should choose.

She wasn't giving him something that was unusual, but something that is found within every female. However, they are not always cultivated within every woman. Make no mistake about it. There are many women like this all over the world. Furthermore, the principles behind the "Virtuous Woman" are deeply rooted in the "Eve Factor," for King Lemuel's mother was essentially telling her son that she knew what values she placed into him and the resulting potential for greatness that he possessed but felt he needed the right woman in his life to make the package complete. She knew, quite well, that if her son got with the right woman that it would do nothing but bring out the wonderful abilities and potential that had been invested in him. He would be guaranteed success.

In her statements you can see how she describes this "Virtuous Woman" as one that gives so much of herself to the man in her life, how safe he would be with her, how she adds value to his name. Truly a Virtuous Woman is aware of her God given abilities and looks for a male that has direction that she can partner up with; for a virtuous woman certainly knows that it is dangerous for her to become involved with a male that is not going anywhere. Above all of this the king's mother draws her son's attention to the Virtuous Woman's value (far above rubies). This shows that she not only wanted her son to desire this type of woman but she also wanted him to appreciate her and cherish her. He would not have to worry about her betraying him or becoming his enemy because not only is her success wrapped up in him, the fact is she also wants him to enjoy the fruits of being secured, successful and satisfied.

SECTION TWO

CAUSES AND ANSWERS

CHAPTER FOUR

CAUSES

For some it does not make sense for a vibrant and healthy female to transform into someone who is totally lost, but unfortunately it is a fact of life that we find, on a daily basis, females in various stages of losing themselves for many different reasons. Let us take the time to examine some of these causes with the purpose of helping her return to her best self.

GIVING AWAY TOO MUCH

The most basic of reasons why a female loses herself is that she gives too much of herself away. As we have stated earlier giving of your Self to others is a noble and wonderful thing, but there are two things you must know. There is a limit at which you can give of yourself and there is a part of you that belongs only to you and God. It doesn't belong to your friends, children, house, business, parents, anything or anyone else, but you and God! When you give that part of you away, then there is nothing remaining of you. Truth is, when you have given that part of you away, everyone has lost you. What happens is you get into a mode where you are not taking time with yourself and end up feeling guilty if the thought of doing for self ever crosses your mind. It is quite noble to give of yourself but if you are not careful you will give entirely too much. Remember loving yourself is not selfish it is self-preserving.

FALLING IN LOVE

One of the most vulnerable times in a female's life is when she totally falls head over heels in love. It is at that point where she doesn't see, hear or think clearly. She is wide open to hurt and the loss of self. The reason is that she throws caution to the wind and gives so much of herself without any attention given to danger. She just jumps in with reckless abandon. Usually when she is in this state she readily expresses her whole heart and total love to the object of her affection. When she does this she can easily end up sprawled on the floor with the remnants of several gallons of ice-cream all over her clothing while feeling that she's made a total fool of herself, confused and depressed.

How many times have you seen someone depressed over unrequited love? How many movies, books, seminars, plays, radio and television programs and chat rooms are filled to overflowing with this topic? For this reason many have been so wounded that they have built walls for protection that rival the Great Wall of China. They have poured out their feelings to someone who probably has no clue or concern as to how vulnerable they are. These same people consequently end up crushing or walking over the feelings of their admirers. In some cases these people cannot respond as their admirer would like due to them already being in a committed relationship or aren't aware their admirers exist. Let's take for example our friend Dorothy:

Dorothy has not been in love for many years due to past
hurts from previous relationships that brought her to a place
where she wouldn't allow herself to even think about
becoming involved with anyone. She had been attending
the Fairburn Apostolic Faith Church where they organized
the Community Help Ministries and were responsible for
organizing the clothing, food and visitation teams along
with the heads of these areas. One of the people that she
ended up working closely with was Carlos.

Carlos, who was over the food distribution ministry,
was not necessarily the most eligible bachelor but was a
complete gentleman. He was thoughtful and completely
dedicated to the work of the ministry. He was one that had
no problem making decisions and taking full responsibility
for things, however he needed help getting things organized
in a way that would make the community food distribution
as effective a ministry as it could be. Consequently as he
and Dorothy began working together she was able to see
what things were missing and started putting together a
plan for him. In return he took the initiative to help her with
many things she could not get to.

During the course of them working out the plans,
organizing teams to handle the monthly distributions and
preparation for the next month's drive they started to
become friends with an appreciation of each other's talents
as well as company. One day while going over plans for
reaching the community through the Food Distribution
ministry, Carlos appeared to look different to Dorothy. Not
that he had changed his grooming or anything like that, but
in reality she was seeing him from a totally different light.
She no longer saw the co-worker in the ministry, but saw
him as someone who could possibly be her knight in
shinning armor. It literally caught her off guard and
happened so quickly that she became completely
overwhelmed. Since it had been over ten years since she

had felt anything like this she began to lose her speech, concentration and ability to stay in his presence without totally blushing all over. Suddenly the close proximity in which they worked seemed a bit too uncomfortable and the cologne he always wore became a bit too appealing. Realizing that these feelings were too much for her to bear she excused herself from his presence.

You see it is easy to fall in love with someone with whom you have a close relationship. They are the people who receive you just as you are and with whom you have no reservation in simply being yourself. It breeds an environment where the two of you can become quite comfortable and dependent on each other's abilities as well as friendship. As some put it "nothing fits as well as a comfortable old shoe." Over a period of time the idea of "what if" seem to seep into our thoughts. Sometimes we dismiss them and other times we entertain them and then there are times when they overtake us as in the case of Dorothy's feelings towards Carlos. How did their relationship end up? Well let's look at the possibilities of such a situation.

Dorothy could spill her guts letting Carlos know the fullness of her feelings towards him and he may not have the same feelings or he may have feelings for her but not as intense. Either way it could very well end up bad for Dorothy. Why? It is very dangerous for you to let anyone know the debts of your love for them; this is how many females are totally taken advantage of. Whenever you expose yourself in this manner, however innocently, that other individual may have your whole heart unconditionally. Males need to feel that they've done something to acquire your love and when it is given to them on a silver platter they sometimes do not appreciate or value it as much as they would if there were a little struggle in acquiring it. This often results in them having someone else on the side because they know that you are simply going to be there.

I realize that some of you want to finish Dorothy's story, but right now that is not as important as understanding what can happen to you when you fall headlong into love with someone. How many times have you seen a female leave their families, drop long time friendships, neglect responsibilities and lose sight of everything that is important to them simply to run behind someone who they are in love with? I am certainly not advocating abstaining from being in love. Neither am I against the feelings of being in love, it's the most wonderful experiences one can have. Those feelings are, in my opinion, to be embraced. I just don't believe that you should run out and tell the individual the depths of these feelings for them. Our emotions can certainly implode on us if we haven't experienced this before or haven't experienced them in a long time, so you need to protect yourself. What if the other person is married, not interested in you at all, homosexual or simply not the right person for you at all? You need to be able to think logically especially when those emotions are going wild.

Believe me you cannot, will not and have no desire whatsoever to risk coming down from that euphoric feeling by being sensible! You are out of control! You're daydreaming, making all kinds of plans and seeing a million different scenarios working out in your mind. On the other hand, you are driving yourself crazy wondering what will happen if he doesn't feel the same way that you feel about him, having all kinds of anxieties whenever you see him, thinking "does he know how I'm feeling about him" and driving yourself crazy trying to determine how to express yourself to him. Adding to this are the people you share this with; sometimes those that you share this with don't understand your entire situation. Other times, they may be very envious of your experience. Regardless of how they feel you must be sure that you guard your heart because you are not in total control and are in need of those that truly care about you (preferably relatives) to help you get through these crazy emotions while allowing you to enjoy the bliss of the moment.

THINKING IT CAN'T BE DONE WITHOUT YOU
Time and again when females, due to frustration, take over responsibilities that are not being handled; they end up over doing it to the point that they lose themselves. Sometimes it is when a male doesn't handle the bills correctly. In this case she will take over the bills and literally worry herself into sickness since there are not enough funds to pay for them. And when the male finally arrives to the place where he can handle them, she has such a chokehold on them as well as other responsibilities that she doesn't trust him enough to let him handle them.

There are cases where the children aren't doing as they should in life and what does the female do? She supports them to the point where they become crippled and she becomes lost. Since she is doing all of the supporting they see no need to ever get out there in life and make it on their own, while she is being totally burnt out and frustrated at their apparent laziness. There are those who become enablers to those who have bad habits be it drugs, alcohol or whatever. Some get so caught up with doing everything and giving so much that they honestly think that if they don't do it nobody will. Sweetheart, believe me if you died today those same people will figure out what they need to do. Literal miracles have happened when people stop doing for others what they can do for themselves. Let God be God! You are not God! Let children grow up and let a man be a man.

WITCHCRAFT/DOMINATION
(Controlling relationships)

Did I say witchcraft? Normally, we think of witchcraft as casting spells over people, but when someone exercises total control over another person's life and not allow them to use own will, then that is considered witchcraft in all of its ugliness. Ladies and gentlemen, God only intended that we dominate things, not people. Whenever anyone seems to be systematically separating you from the people you care about, please recognize that this person has all intention of dominating you. I am not talking about falling in love and not having time for everyone as you normally would, but a blatant removal of those you care about through manipulation and bad advice given by the perpetrator in an attempt to alienate you. Why? It is so that you will be without anyone who can give you proper input regarding your relationship. Get the message this is about CONTROL. This gives the other person the ability to make you feel that you have no one to turn to but him or her in your life giving them much power over you. Whether you see it this way or not this is witchcraft that has the ability to cause you to lose yourself without realizing it. This sort of thing is exactly what has left many females abused (physically, mentally and emotionally), lost and unfortunately in worst cases dead.

MISUNDERSTANDING TRADITIONAL ROLES
(Being one doesn't mean you are not an individual)

Shelters are filled with women whose husbands or boyfriends believe that the female was suppose to do anything he tells her and that she was created to serve him. They think that when the Bible said that he should rule over her (Genesis 3:16) that the intentions were that he should do this with an iron fist upside her head if she showed any sign of self-will. Unfortunately there are many that are of this mindset who have consequently done, in some cases, irreparable damage to our sisters, physically and emotionally. While the Scriptures teach that when a man finds a wife he's found a good thing; we must understand that a female is not a thing.

The thing that he has found is the relationship and within a relationship there are two individuals with varied opinions, ideas and perspectives that bring many wonderful flavors to it. To cause one of them to lose their individuality is to damage the relationship. For to lose oneself is also to diminish the love that one has for themselves; when that takes place the relationship is no longer two-sided it becomes one sided where someone is going to feel cheated, unappreciated or used.

I am reminded of a time when my wife was over the children's department of our church and seemed to be more recognized than I was. One of the brothers and I were talking and during the conversation he just happen to bring up the subject as if I needed to put my wife in check, as if my manhood was in danger. You see my wife is very talented and extremely creative and one of the best organizers I have ever seen. If she organizes something you can best believe that it will be a success. She took a four member children's choir and turned it to a very successful seventy-two-member choir, organized trips to apple farms, petting zoos, roller skate events, and plays. The brother mentioned the many positive things my wife was doing and how her name was upon everyone's lips. I looked at him understanding exactly what he was trying to say. I asked him what name they were using when they mentioned her name. He said "Minister Walters' wife."

I again asked him what name they were using. He again said "Minister Walters's wife." I then told him how much she enjoyed directing and organizing the children's choir and their activities. I also mentioned how I would sometimes hold my youngest daughter in my lap while she worked. Finally, I explained to him how I had to suffer with a woman who would come home feeling great about herself and happy that her husband gives her space to exercise her many talents. Yeah I had to suffer with all of the blessings that came from me allowing her to continue being the woman I fell in love with. Needless to say he didn't feel my pain, but wished he could.

In our twenty plus years together we have learned to allow each other to have our own identities and it has greatly enriched our love for each other. I don't know about anyone else but I love falling in love with my wife over and over and over again. Understand that God's Word complements relationships and leaves lots of room for individuality while at the same time blends them to the point that they become one in the process.

THINKING THAT YOU CAN CHANGE HIM

The problem is that many women come into a relationship knowing that a given male has issues but feel that they can change him and, worse yet, that he is willing to let you change him. This type of thinking can only lead to frustration, emptiness and the state of being lost.

COMMUNICATION PROBLEMS

Regardless of what language we speak there is yet found in every language the dialect of the male and female that has the ability to bring further confusion to our ability to communicate with one another. What does communication have to do with a female losing herself? Everything! However, we want to focus on how not being able to interpret the language can lead to frustration and disappointment, which can lead her to this path. Let's peek into some typical situations and conversations and see how this can develop:

What She Means When She Says….

In an effort to slow up the process of a female losing herself, we must understand that males and females communicate differently in spite of the fact that they are speaking the same language. Because of this she may be attempting to communicate things to the male that he totally does not understand causing frustration over a period of time and contributing to her losing herself. Have you ever heard a woman say, "Men are clueless?" The truth of the matter is not that they are clueless but that women and men may speak the same language, but their expressions often have different meanings.

Below there's a number of them with their interpretation. This is not written to insult or belittle either sex but it is intended to give tools to accomplish a much better and more enriched relationship through proper communication. When two people understand what the other person is saying, then there is a better chance of them meeting the needs that are being requested.

You don't understand what I'm going through

You don't love me anymore

You aren't listening to me

In all three of these statements she is saying a little bit more than the obvious. These statements and many others like them are ways in which she is trying to get your attention. Evidently she feels that you need to spend some time with her or romance her. Take the time to talk and listen to her, allow her to exhale with the absence of television, the newspaper and any other distraction. Make sure that she has you undivided attention. If it seems that you are not understanding what she is trying to communicate, then tell her what you think she is saying and allow her to fully explain it until you are both clear on what is being communicated. Essentially, all she really wants is your time and attention.

You don't need me

She is saying that you are shutting her out in spite of all her efforts to be there for you. For example, whenever you come home and she asks you how your day went understand that this is one of the ways she feels included in your life. She doesn't necessarily feel that she needs to have the answer but feels that if she is just able to listen to your concerns, then she has been a help to you.

We, as men, are solution oriented while women don't always need for you to have a solution. All she sometime needs is a listening ear. Men, on the contrary, would prefer talking if we can come to a solution to the problem. Given this understanding can you see how we as men make her feel left out when we don't want to talk about our problems? She feels as if you don't need her consoling, comfort or conversation and thus have no need for her. When you allow her in, she then feels more a part of your life. Don't forget, she's your help-meet. As an added note guys I am not saying that you should cry on her shoulders all of the time because then she would see you as weak or less than a man. At the same time when you are sharing difficult things with her please make sure that you let her know that you have a plan that you are working on to resolve the problem otherwise you will have a worrying woman.

You need to be (I want you to be) a man
She is essentially saying that she wants you to be responsible, to take the initiative on things. She doesn't want you to wait on her to suggest or tell you to do something that is your responsibility.

We need to spend some time together
This one is sort of tricky. Guys picture this. You attended church early Saturday morning, spent some time having lunch with some friends, went to a ball game that afternoon with some other couples and when you came home she looked you in the eye and said "we need to spend some time together." Fellows, I know what you are thinking. You were with her all day long, so what does she mean we need to spend some time together?

Well what she is actually saying is that she wants the two of you to take some personal time to communicate, specifically talk. She needs to talk and feel connected to you on an emotional and spiritual level. You need to shoot the television, burn the newspaper and allow the children (if you have any) to destroy the house if necessary so that the two of you can communicate. She needs your undivided attention. Hold her hand and listen to her. Let her know that she is a priority. This allows her to get in tune with you and also gives her the opportunity to express whatever is on her mind. It is healthy for her and absolutely necessary for the health of your relationship. If you do not do this she may start acting a bit edgy and somewhat mistrusting towards you but you won't know why. What is even stranger than that is she probably won't know either. By the way spending time must be done in person and cannot be done over the phone. Ladies, males often think that if you are talking on the phone that you are spending time. So if you don't want to spend time on the phone, you had better make your conversations short.

No I don't want to talk about it

Guys this is another one of those opposite statements. First, you need to know that whenever something is wrong with her she thinks that you actually know what's wrong. For that reason she will be angry with you and treat you as if you already know but are either ignoring it or are being selfish. [By the way ladies we don't always know what's wrong. A note before I get to the meat of the subject at hand; guys always be prepared to apologize even if you are not wrong. Remember we are supposed to love them as Christ loved the church and GAVE HIMSELF for them (Ephesians 5:25). Suck it up and say I'm sorry so that communication can continue.]

When you see that she is upset with you and you have no idea why, you've asked her if she wants to talk about it and get the response "no, I don't want to talk about it", please understand (as long as she is not throwing a frying pan at you) she DOES WANT TO TALK ABOUT IT. What she is communicating to you is that she wants you to pursue her and let her know that she is worth pursuing. Again, this shows that you value her. If you simply walk away you are saying that she is not worth the extra effort and that you may not care, so pursue!

The following are situations where she is asking for help or making a request of the male:

I'm tired

This usually occurs when she is doing a multitude of things or a task that has to get done now. What she is saying is I have got to get this done and I need your help. She is looking for you to ask her how you might be of assistance.

One scenario is she may be folding clothes, cooking the dinner and helping the children with their homework. She needs to get all of them done, but cannot do them all. She'll say "I'm tired!" She is simply asking you to step in and give her a hand.

Hinting: Females often think that males know what they are thinking or experiencing. Therefore, instead of directly telling us what they want, think or feel they give us hints. Sometimes they leave things around the house as clues to what they may want for their birthdays or some other special occasion believing that the male is going to know what message she is sending. Unfortunately, giving a male a hint often ends up sounding, in his mind, like the request may not be important or serious. Therefore, it often does not get the proper response. Ladies please do yourself and the males in your life a favor use the direct approach. The following are situations where she is hinting that she wants the male to handle something:

A cruise might be a fun vacation next year
She definitely wants to go on a cruise next year and would like for you to make the reservations and get the tickets. Please understand that she wants you to take charge of making the reservations. She does not want to make the reservations. In her mind part of the excitement/romance of going is you making the preparations. It also says that you want to do this with her. Oh don't worry; she will do the shopping but you need to handle the reservations and get things started! When he hears her say that a cruise MIGHT BE a fun vacation next year; he hears MIGHT BE as not being a definite, necessary or needed thing. He hears it as a nice to have or maybe.

I think I have/I think the car may have a flat tire
Instead of asking you to fix the flat tire she is giving you a hint. What she is really saying to you is "would you please fix my flat tire?" or "would you please check out the car?"

The garage door won't close
Again she is asking you to do something. In this case she is asking you to go out to the garage door, examine it and if it needs repair to fix it.

I think the sink is stopped up
That's right. I think you've got it. She wants you to fix the sink.

Note: There's a funny thing about broken things around the house and women. When something around the house is broken males find ways to live with it until he finds time to either fix it or have it fixed. Females, on the other hand, find it very difficult to do this because it is as if the house is a part of who she is. It is like leaving a part of her broken or undone. This is why she is constantly asking you; when are you going to fix it. In situations like this it is important to give her an exact date and actually stick to it. Don't give her a date or time and then don't do it. If you do you will be building a case for her to begin losing trust in you. Dependability is major in a relationship. If you want to be her hero, take care of the things that need to be fixed or handled!

What She Thinks When You Say….
How many times have you heard of a well meaning man who has tried to be a caring, concerned and supportive, but ends up mistakenly saying the wrong things to the lady in his life? In spite of his desire to help he seems to blunder when it comes to saying the right thing. The woman ends

up in an even worse condition than she was prior to him attempting to help. He's now standing there feeling like an idiot and even worse frustrated because he was simply trying to help and now he has made it worse. He doesn't know what do and is even more confused as to what is wrong with the lady in his life. As we've stated earlier it is simply a matter of language and knowing how the female perceives certain phrases and actions. No she's not crazy and no he's not totally clueless. They are simply, if we can put it that way, two opposite genders that speak, feel and perceive things differently. Whenever there are two people who speak different languages attempting to communicate, they will not comprehend each other without interpretation. So let's see if we can help a brother out by bringing a little clarity to the fogginess of the situation:

I don't know what's wrong with you. What's the matter with you?
In this situation she may not know what is wrong either but that's not the point. She doesn't always need for you to know what's wrong. In fact she doesn't even need for you to fix it all of the time. What she needs is to know that you care; for you to be there for her listening and allowing her to express herself without interruption or resolution. The idea of you being there for her without the need to quickly come to a resolution expresses to her that she means something to you and that you are ready to now make her the focus. You'll be doing for her what she has been doing for you (which, by the way, may have contributed to getting her to this point in the first place). This doesn't have to make sense to you, but for a female sometimes just being able to express herself freely allows the healing process to begin. In fact it may actually help her figure out what is wrong. However, when you say the above she feels that you don't want to understand and feels devalued by you.

I'm going to give you some space
The only thing she hears at that point is that you are going to leave her. You are dumping her. She's not worth going through the struggle and you are not willing to see her through her difficult time. Sometimes she's hearing that you really do have someone else that is more important to you than her. (Could it be the other woman?) Instead of doing this take the time to remove yourself from the equation and tell her that you need a minute or two to gather yourself, take a deep breath and sit down. Then tell her to continue because you are prepared to give her your full attention (without being defensive).

Look I'm going to take a walk and I'll be right back when you calm down.
The only thing she can hear at the point of you taking a short walk is that IT'S OVER, "INFIDELITY", "DIVORCE' and "HE'S LEAVING ME!" Whenever a woman is in a condition like this, for goodness sakes DO NOT LEAVE! The message you are conveying is that you want out of the relationship and have no desire whatsoever in trying to work things out. I know it seems logical that maybe she needs a break or breathing room, but believe me at that moment you need to stay! What she needs at that moment is to know that you are not going anywhere, but are there for her no matter what it takes.

We're growing apart
Elvis has left the building! Not only are you thinking about breaking up you've already got your bags packed in her mind. Instead of saying that, why not ask her where she thinks the relationship is and what sort of things you both can do to strengthen the relationship. Let her know that you are not asking her to be critical of you, but inform her that

you want the relationship to continue growing and getting better. The object is to inform her that you are aware of problems within the relationship, yet you are committed enough to work through whatever problems that exist to make your relationship even stronger.

Negative Speech, Jesting & Joking

How many times have you seen people say negative things to one another in the name of just having fun who end up severely hurting the other person, break out in an argument or even a fight? How many times have you seen someone totally destroy another person's confidence through this foolishness? Let me tell you something, WORDS WILL HURT YOU! People have lost their total self-esteem through negative talk from others and especially from themselves. Psychiatrist's offices are filled with people who have suffered from such nonsense. Marriages have been done irreparable damaged as a result of "having a little fun." The Scripture says that jesting and joking is not suitable for us (Ephesians 5:4) and as such shouldn't be used with our loved ones. I never, and I mean NEVER crack jokes or make fun of my wife especially in public. I respect her too much. The other danger is when you continue speaking to someone in a negatively, you inadvertently end up treating them that way. Ladies be aware of this and do not allow any male or anyone for that matter to use the wrong terminology or tone when communicating with you!

OTHER CAUSES

YOU CAN'T BE HIS MAMA
(even if you did give birth to him)

Earlier we talked about the part of you that only belongs to you and God. It is a thin line between being a great HELP-

MEET and giving too much of yourself to the male in your life. A good man doesn't want or need quite that much of you. He wants you to be dependent on him but not to the extent of being clingy. He wants you to be supportive but there is also a thin line between being supportive and being his mama. Even if you are his mama there is a time when you need to allow a man to be a man. There has been so much talk about stroking a male's ego and how sensitive it is, but this needs to be clearly defined otherwise you will become totally frustrated trying to motivate and help a man who has no intention of going anywhere or doing anything.

I have seen many women stuck with a man that has been living on his mama and any other woman who would be foolish enough to support him. I have seen mothers do so much for their sons that they have made weak knee, jelly-back, lazy, shiftless specimens of useless manhood out of them. They are no good for themselves and a detriment to any female that comes into contact with them. Ladies, whatever you do please avoid at all cost this type of male! Don't forget that you have an innate desire to help the male achieve and getting involved with this type of male has the ability to totally destroy you!

Find someone who is going somewhere, has plans and is working towards accomplishing them. There is a special feeling a man has when he has provided for his own and handled his responsibilities that must not be taken away from him. When you've found a man is on his way to achieving a worthy goal, you've found a happy man as well as someone who may be worthy of your EVABILITIES. Whenever you find a male that has no direction, motivation or desire to move forward in life; he is not worthy of a woman's sympathy, encouragement or support. In fact that is not what he needs at all. What he really needs is a good dose of reality or a swift kick where the sun doesn't shine! A male in this condition is of no good use to a woman until he comes to himself and assumes responsibility for his own actions or inaction.

This situation has nothing to do with you as a woman and you need to know that you cannot change anyone but yourself. If you do not come to terms with this type of a situation, it will bring you nothing but misery, frustration and unhappiness. Women married to men like this end up having great disrespect and eventually view him with disgust! Now don't get me wrong. I am not saying that a man that doesn't have a specific direction is in that category, nor am I saying that if he is discouraged that you should kick him when he is down. Some men have desire and motivation but no clear direction. Others have a clear direction and motivation but no knowledge of how to get there. Both of these men deserve your encouragement. They also need to feel safe to express their ideas to you without being laughed at or made to feel emasculated after talking to you. This type of male simply needs for you to believe in him. So express it. When he is discouraged give him that little boost and, believe me, he'll go after his dreams like a thirsty deer panting after water. Your encouragement should not preclude you from being helpful when listening to his plans; for they are not just his plans they also affect and involve you. He needs your insight, concerns and suggestions, you also need to express yourself and not be a silent partner. Just make sure that he understands that YOU ARE NOT AGAINST THE PLAN. Ladies, for God's sake, your sake and especially for the male's sake, stop being his mama! In other words: LET A MAN BE A MAN.

THINKING HE KNOWS WHEN HE DOESN'T

"Doesn't he get it?" "Men are so stupid!" "They don't know anything!" "Do I have to tell him everything?" "You know what's wrong!" Ladies how many times have you made any of these statements to or about men? Have you ever made any of these assumptions? I know you have. However, I want to inform you that honestly, HE DOESN'T KNOW!

One of the greatest frustrations a female has is when things seem so obvious to her and at the same time so incredibly oblivious to the male in her life. Whenever something is blatantly obvious to us we always assume that it should also be clear to everyone else. For this reason we sometimes respond negatively to them. There are several circumstances in the lives of males and females where this occurs. For example; whenever a female is upset with a male they actually think that the male knows exactly why she is upset. Ladies, HE DOESN'T KNOW.

Brothers she thinks you know what the problem is, so explain to her that you would truly like to get things right, but are not sure what you've done. Then there's the situation where she pulls away and says she doesn't want to talk or be bothered when in reality she wants him to pursue her. Ladies, HE DOESN'T KNOW.

Brothers as long as she is not throwing a skillet at you, she actually wants you to pursue her. By doing this you show her that she is worth whatever effort it takes to get things right with her. If she says that nothing is wrong and at the same time giving you obvious signs that all is not well in HAPPYVILLE, well then you need to pursue and find out what's wrong.

It takes time to build a successful relationship but the results are more than worth it. So remember, you wouldn't call someone who didn't speak your language stupid for not heeding your warning to duck out of the way of a baseball bat heading towards their head. Therefore neither should we look at one another in that light when we see or know things they do not. As a woman you have been given this gift, but what good is it if you don't know what it is for and how to use it? The woman was created to be the perfect help for the man. That is why you know things that appear to be so obvious to you and totally obscure to him. Otherwise you could not help him achieve. Embrace that thought. I must however reiterate that you do not need to baby sit him or be his mama. Also you cannot help someone who refuses to be helped. If you attempt to do that you'll end up becoming completely frustrated and possibly losing yourself. So make sure that you are able to couple this with a little wisdom. If the male is willing to hear and be helped by trying to understand and see what he doesn't see, be patient with him because the rewards are more than worth it.

BEING A WIFE TOO SOON

A dollar earned is much more appreciated than one that has been given. I have seen so many women end up being totally lost and left out in the cold after believing that if they do all of the wifely duties for their male prior to even getting engaged that he will surely love, cherish and without any doubt whatsoever marry them. They are truly fooling themselves.

Haven't you heard that if he gets the milk for free that he doesn't have to buy the cow? No I am not calling anyone a heifer. What I am saying is that there is a time when a woman is obligated to participate in the relationship as a wife and it is not prior to marriage. I would even go as far as saying that you should not totally reveal or give your whole heart until you are engaged and even then you should reserve some for after he says "I DO" or "I WILL." Just in case someone doesn't get it. I mean AFTER the marriage ceremony. Prior to that you should not be washing his clothes, picking up his laundry, cleaning his apartment or home, cooking all of his meals and oh yeah giving him all of the sex his heart desires! If you are doing all of this, then what are you going to do when and if he marries you? What will he have to look forward to? You don't want him to become so comfortable with you that you are taken for granted. In other words, he needs to have reminders that you may be here now, but there is the possibility that you will not be there if he doesn't make the proper moves. Years after we were married I found out that my wife had made up in her mind that she was not going to continue dating me for a long period of time without a commitment. In fact she felt that going past two years was entirely too much time out of her life. If I couldn't figure out that I wanted to marry her by then, she was going to see her way out of that relationship. I'm sure glad that I proposed before the two years were up. You've got to give him something to run after. Men need the pursuit without feeling that you are playing games with them. When there are clearly defined borders/limitations coupled with realness, it lets him know that you value yourself and that he should do the same. It also lets him know that the lady that he is with is special.

The limitations also tell him that there is much more in the relationship for him to look forward to if he does what is required. Some things have to be earned and there are parts of you that deserve to be preserved so that you will be cherished not used. I know someone is thinking that, "if I don't, someone else will." That is exactly what is wrong with men today. Too many women have let down their standards. There was a time where a male could not get a date unless he had a car and a job. When females stood up and demanded this, the males somehow figured out how to get a job and miraculously purchased a car. Why? It is because when a male is interested in a female, he is willing to invest in her. He is willing to do whatever it takes.

Ladies, do not forget that you also have the gift of influence. If the male you are with is not willing to respect your limitations until a ring is on your finger and you have removed your wedding veil, then you are with the wrong male. He is not going to respect you regardless of what you do. Oh no! Are you still singing that same old song of if I don't somebody will? Okay, let's look at what that somebody ends up with. She has a track star. That's right, she has someone who will run through her money, her girlfriends, her sisters, her property and anything else she allows. Some of these women end up moving in with the male; having his babies and regret years later that he never gave her his name or worse than that he has been doing other women the same way. Other times, her life gets left on hold for so long that when he has no where else to turn from a life of living off of other women he returns to her with a disease or absolutely nothing to offer. Then there's the one who is so grateful to have him that she is willing to share him with however many women (or men) he desires. If you do not respect yourself, you are directing the male in your life to disrespect you and are opening up the door for abuse. If he wants a wife let him marry you. Otherwise you are setting yourself up for great disappointment.

WHAT MAKES HER STAY LOST?

Okay we have discussed what some of the things are that cause her to lose her self-worth and end up in the state that we refer to as lost, now we need to look at a few things that could cause her to stay there:

Not Knowing

Many women are not aware that they are lost. Sometimes she is incapable of telling anyone what she's feeling or going through because she doesn't know herself. It is important to allow her to simply exhale all that is in her heart without attempting to fix it for her. It is through this process that she may come to terms with the fact that she is lost, what she is feeling and experiencing. Using the list of symptoms given in chapter one can be quite helpful in recognizing where she is. By the way, I do not advise males to read them off to her when she is in this state. It would not be a good idea, as she most likely would not receive it in a positive manner from him. That in itself is different conversation altogether.

Guilt

Sometimes females get religious beliefs confused and end up staying in negative situations because she thinks it is God's will that she give all that she is and to not do this would be selfish. Many of them misunderstand the scripture that teaches us to love others and do not comprehend that they should first learn to care for and love themselves, which gives them the basis for loving others. In the case of religious women being in bad relationships many times their family members place guilt upon them thinking that they are encouraging her to stay in a bad situation believing that it is not God's will for them to separate.

For those that believe in the Bible, I say that you need to know that there is an allowance in the Scripture for separation (I Corinthians 7:10-11). Unfortunately, there are times when it is necessary. We are not without flaws and when we find that our partner has abuse issues, regardless to where they come from, we must take the time to get the proper help. Those that are victims of it need to realize that they need to allow the victimizers get help by removing yourself from the equation. The reality is that there are times when it calls for us to use separation to protect the innocent and also heal the sick. This can often bring on a lot of undeserved guilt precluding her from finding herself again.

Guilt also finds its way into deceiving her into believing that if she takes the time to care for herself that other will not survive. How many of you out there have mothers who constantly enable children with their bad habits and irresponsible lifestyles? Sisters I want you to know that everyone will survive if you learn to love upon you. In fact, you will be empowering others to grow in areas that you have been hindering them from. That's right you have probably smothered them with all of the well meaning love and care you give. The sad part is that you are probably your worst victim. Do them and yourself a favor; let go and let God! What do I mean? Chances are you are holding on to what is more comfortable and familiar in fear of moving into what may be an unknown. You know, asking questions to yourself like "if I don't... who will take care of it?", "if I step out and try this how will I survive?" and things like What if I don't make it?" The stepping out of this situation is the "letting go" and believing that somehow and some way you'll make it is the act of faith that "lets God" do his part. This act of faith is necessary for living. That's right I said live! Jesus came that you might live life to its fullest (John 10:10).

The main idea for this chapter is for us to recognize that there are reasons that a female loses herself so that we may take the necessary steps to alleviate them helping her find her way back to the beautiful being that Jesus created.

CHAPTER FIVE

TIME FOR REPLENISHMENT

Now that we've totally dragged the male and female through the proverbial mud, it is time to get to the process of repairing the damage we've all played a part in. We've all looked into the container after pouring out the last few drops of whatever libation we were thirsty for and uttered, "Aren't there a few drops left?" No my brothers and sisters there is nothing left and if you do not replenish the container there never will be! It is time to again make the Kool-Aid.

TAKE TIME FOR SELF

Ladies, you need to take some quiet time. Quiet time is an occasion for self, which allows you to be introspective and rejuvenate. Take a moment to think because what you have been doing has not allowed you time to do so. It is so vital to your well being that you simply breathe. This allows you to go back to how you were prior to this situation and gives you room to again, or for the first time, know yourself. Ask yourself what it was that you enjoyed doing before all of this. What was it that made you happy, what made you feel good? Life is much too short to rush through doing everything except loving and enjoying the person that Jesus created. Stop at some point in your day (or begin your day) alone listening to yourself think. Get rid of all of the interruptions like television, radio, people, work and whatever else that would hinder you from hearing your own thoughts.

If you have to get up a little earlier, do it. Grab yourself a nice cup of chamomile tea and relax. Gather your thoughts and listen to the voices in your head so that you may know what you are feeling and experiencing. Cuddle up with a favorite book and get lost in it. Draw yourself a nice bath and just soak for about an hour (or two) laying your head back with your eyes closed as you take pleasure in the serenity of the moment. Pull out those skin care products you've been promising yourself you were some day going to use to treat yourself with and finally give yourself a long awaited and deserved facial. Look in that mirror and see that gorgeous hunk of a woman that you are. You know she's beautiful! Look if no one else is telling you wonderful things about you, then you had better get busy telling it to yourself. Tell yourself that you are a wonderful person. Admit to yourself that you deserve great things and that this time that you are taking is WELL OVER DUE! Say it out loud with emotion. If anyone says that you shouldn't talk to yourself just take the notion that I borrowed from someone else. I like talking to intelligent people and I like hearing intelligent people talk. Manicure those nails and maybe while you're at it, take a few extra minutes to pamper yourself a little more. YOU DESERVE IT! This is the beginning of you giving you back to yourself. Let the house explode if necessary, but get that time in.

Guys help give her back to herself. Find a way to free her up so that she has time to do this. Encourage her to take this personal time by doing simple things like:

1. Purchasing bath and beauty products for her;
2. Handling some of her responsibilities so that she will have free time;
3. Take the children, give her some money and let her know that you want to give her a break;
4. Purchasing a package from a day spa if that's something she would like;
5. Draw a luxurious bath for her with all of the amenities waiting for her to enjoy;
6. Tell her that you appreciate all of the wonderful things that she has been doing and would like for her to enjoy a leisurely break for the day as you serve her for a change, or;
7. Give her a few extra dollars and tell her that she deserves to go shopping and remind her only to buy for herself.

Please tell her that you recognize all that she does and have great appreciation for it, but don't want her to totally wear out. Through these things not only do you help her replenish, but you also bring honor to her (I Peter 3:7). You are beginning to restore value to her and as you know when a female loses herself what she really loses mostly is self-value. So lady, take out some woman time for yourself. Give yourself some long deserved TLC.

REMEMBERING HAPPINESS
One of the common denominators that I have found in females who have lost themselves is that in their desire to do so much for someone else they have forgotten what it is that makes them happy. This is particularly true in abused

females. They are so busy trying to please someone else and concerned about what they might think or say that they no longer remember what it is like to do something that is a total joy to no one else but them. So many have had hobbies, talents, a passion to achieve one thing or another, but have long since forsaken these special things that make them unique.

Stop right this minute and ask yourself what it is that you like. What makes you happy? What would you like to accomplish? If you had the time to do it, what would you do? Are there any fun things regardless how small someone else may think it is that you simply adore? Whatever it is, begin to embrace it in your heart this very moment because it is part of your inner beauty. It is the ability to dream that gives us hope and in many cases a reason to live. And you need to live! Don't forget Jesus came that you should have life more abundantly (John 10:10). Now I am not suggesting you to run away and abandon everything and everybody. Simply that you awaken the joy that once resided within. Awaken the fact that you are a person with dreams that mean something to you and if they mean something to you they are important. Even if it is rolling around in the grass kicking your legs up in the air while laughing and screaming at the top of your voice, go ahead and do it! It will help you again find you.

LOVING SELF FIRST

How do we love ourselves first without becoming self-centered? Is it all right to first take care of me and then take care of others? This is often the dilemma of a female lost. She has either never had or has lost her compass that speaks to truly loving others.

The following comes from our newsletter (go to www.stevewaltersministries.com) entitled "Love The One

You're With" We have included it to help you in finding that compass:

Most of us clearly understand God's command that we love others (Matthew 22:39), but unfortunately some of us don't realize that this has to first begin with love for ourselves. Oh yes we can name the Greek words for love with great pride as they roll off of our tongue "Philios, Storge, Eros and Agape", but when it comes to loving ourselves we sometimes come up short. One cannot properly love someone else if they don't love themselves. Loving one self is the basis on which we are able to love others. It is also that which helps us know the boundaries of that love. That's why we are taught to love others as (we first love) ourselves. This principle helps us maintain a healthy balance when it comes to love. In other words you don't love someone to the point of smothering them or hurting yourself. People who do not maintain self love can: forgive others, but find difficulty forgiving self, see worth in others, but not in themselves, find time to do good for others and little or no time for themselves, give compliments to others, but find it hard to receive them, see others as lovable, but themselves as unlovable. Furthermore it seems that we become confused with the scripture that tells us to deny ourselves (Matthew 16:24). Some of us think it tells us to neglect ourselves. The denying of us, as spoken by the scripture, is neglecting and forsaking our ways of doing, viewing and pursuing and embracing God's ways of doing, viewing and pursuing. For instance we tend to curse those that curse us, but God's way is to bless them that curse us and pray for them that despitefully use us (Luke 6:28). It is trading in of our old ways to embrace His ways and has nothing to do with treating ourselves bad. Loving yourself is self-preserving and not selfish or self centered. It causes us to protect ourselves and thereby survive. That's why we are taught to "save ourselves" (Acts 2:40). So before you run out there and love someone else; make sure that you already "Love The One You're With!"

The real question that needs to be asked is not if you love someone else but whether you really love your Self.

ADDRESSING A WOMAN'S GREATEST NEED

Of all the things a woman desires from the males in her life the greatest is to know that she is loved and cared for. This covers provision, protection and everything else. It especially applies to married couples. Look at these Scriptures in the Bible:

a) Ephesians 5:25 shows self sacrifice and a sincere eagerness to grow with and commit to the relationship;

b) Ephesians 5:28-29 show unselfishness, consideration, provision and protection. It also shows both sides of the male (steel & velvet) in the relationship, and;

c) Ephesians 5:31 demonstrates an understanding of the proper priority of responsibilities in the relationship.

When helping the female replenish always remember her greatest need and reassure her that you are committed to her.

TONE, TOUCH & TOGETHERNESS

Brothers whenever a female is in the state of being lost it is important for you to sensitive to the tone of your voice, the tenderness of your touch and togetherness in your conversation. Make sure that you touch her physically and emotionally with gentleness and that your conversation conveys togetherness. Your words are crucial, so be more ready to listen. Don't forget that she may not know exactly what is wrong herself, so be prepared to listen without trying to immediately fix things. Don't raise your voice but if you do speak let it be with words that express that to her that whatever it takes you are willing to go through it with her. This is a good time to hold her hand or embrace her to add to your reassurance. I must reiterate that it is so important that you do more listening than talking because a female needs to express herself during these times. Don't worry about her blaming you for whatever may have gone bad in her life; just make sure that your tone of voice and action are those that speak to caring, interest and togetherness.

Your willingness to commit to the relationship is much more important than your pride. Who knows? You may very well be the problem but your willingness to stick with her will certainly outweigh any blame or silly sense of pride. If she is stating that she doesn't want to talk and is pulling away from you, pursue. As long as she is not throwing things at you it is safe to pursue her. In fact, she actually wants you to pursue her. She wants you to tell her by your pursuit that she is valuable to you and more than worth the effort.

Guys, I know this sounds stupid but please believe me its true. Despite her saying she doesn't want to talk about it – don't forget they speak a different language – she means "pursue me, show me I'm worth it!" It may be a good idea to have her get dressed and take her out so that she will see that you are genuinely interested in listening to her and getting through whatever ails her. That is a wonderful way to make many a female feel valued and ready to talk.

THE ISSUE OF TRUST

Trust that has been broken may never be given again, but there is the possibility of it being earned. If you've ever broken a person's trust, you shouldn't expect them to simply trust you again. It is not that simple a thing to do. Trusting a person requires that you open up to being let down, hurt, deceived and betrayed and when this is experienced it can be very painful or even devastating. For this reason, the person affected should not expect to immediately feel as if they can trust again. They should give themselves time to heal and to understand what took place. At the same time, the one who broke the trust should not expect that person to immediately trust them, but should have a commitment to do what it takes to earn the trust while respecting the other person's dilemma, pain and new boundaries. You also need to take the time to truly understand what happen and become empathetic or sympathetic to the person you've injured. Neither of you should put a set time on the healing, but allow time to heal the wounds between you both as you grow in this newfound relationship.

I FORGIVE (Them & Myself)

Whether you do it consciously or not; forgiveness is absolutely necessary for replenishment. Many people shy away from forgiving for two reasons. One is that they fear facing the truth. No one readily wants to admit that they have either been very foolish or have allowed this to happen to them because it is a very painful thing to view you as being that weak or depraved. Shame is often associated with admitting to oneself what has happened and contributes to the difficulty of dealing with that which has occurred. It is often easier to pretend that it never happened. How many times have we heard of repressed memories suddenly resurfacing in a person's life? Our minds are so incredible that we seem to have totally erased those bad experiences out of our mind until they have brought on bad reactions in our lives that we and or others have to deal with. By the time we have figured out what happened we have ruined several relationships and are wondering why we can't be happy. That's what happens to people who move directly from one relationship to another without allowing themselves to look at what went wrong in the first one. (It is important to take that time so that we may look at what happened, deal with it and move on.)

Sometimes you need to journal or write down your feelings regardless to how terrible they are. This can be of great benefit because most of the time we have no idea how we are feeling and through this process we can flesh them out. Now if you are angry with someone please do not show them your writings or even approach them. This is about you and not them. Read what you have written and if you've left anything out, finish it. Go back and read it again. This may take as long as a month or more, but however long it takes it is worth it. It's not an easy process because it will bring out a lot of pain, so if you are not ready for it take your time and ease into it. Don't be afraid to cry or feel bad for yourself. Your body and mind were built to handle it. You don't need to medicate yourself. You need to feel your pain as well as your joy. When you've read and have no more to write, take the journal to the toilet with you and literally flush those issues, strongholds and past out of your life. As you go through this process tell yourself that you are better than that and deserve better. Thank God for bringing you to a place where you can know this within the depth of your very inner being. Through this process you will, of course, experience a lot of anger, sorrow and pain but you will also experience enlightenment, freedom and peace.

The other reason for avoiding forgiveness is due to the misunderstanding of what forgiveness is. Let me quickly clarify it by saying that forgiveness is not saying that which was done to you is alright, but it is saying that you are no longer holding blame and extracting justice upon those that have committed this injustice on you; even if that person is you. Forgiveness of those who have done wrong to us is the obvious thing, but the importance of and need to forgive is ourselves is often obscure. We don't always realize that we blame ourselves for being victimized. Sometimes the one who has done the abuse leads us to believe that it was totally our fault and after everything is over and we've forgiven everyone involved we find ourselves yet not capable of getting past it. The reason for this is we have not as yet forgiven ourselves.

I want to tell you now that it is all right to forgive yourself. You also need to know that sometimes it isn't necessarily your fault and even if it is you need to forgive you so that you can move on to better things. You now need to treat you better. What does forgiveness do? It allows you to accept what has happened, settle it within yourself and free yourself from the chains of the past allowing you to go forward. Forgiveness gives you back your power to live again. With it you can resume growing and becoming all that you were intended. It also gives you the ability to experience you and all of life again. It does not make what was done to you right, but empowers you to free yourself from being stuck in the past desiring that vengeance is extracted upon the perpetrators. Leave the vengeance to God. He says, vengeance belongs to Him, so let Him handle it. Therefore, embrace forgiveness and release bitterness with all of its toxins. Once you do this you will actually experience a change in your breathing, feel lighter and become a happier you. You'll also be on the road to loving you again.

LEARNING FROM MISTAKES

One of the things we want you to go away with after reading this book is that it is okay to give and okay to receive, but understand clearly that on both sides there are limits. We are not attempting to make anyone feel any worse than they already are, but I do want you to face the mistakes that were made which brought you to this point. Please understand that mistakes are the way we learn. As babies we fall before we learn to walk, we crash before we learn to ride the bicycle and go outside the lines before we finally learn to color.

To avoid facing your mistakes is to not grow and experience life in its fullest. I know of many females who constantly sabotage themselves from receiving so many blessings for fear of making the same mistake. The truth of the matter is the only way to experience love in its fullness is to expose yourself to the possibility of being hurt again. Will you be hurt again? There is a great possibility you will, but those same odds can also bring everything you've ever hoped for and much more. The main thing is to learn from the mistake so that you don't repeat it again and if you do get back up, dust off and try it again. The glory of the accomplishment will outweigh all of your bloopers to the point that they become distant memories. More than anything else you need to get on with your life and life is filled with happy people who made a few so-called dumb mistakes. It is not your first and I promise you it will not be your last, so go ahead and ride that bicycle.

CHAPTER SIX

WHAT MAKES A FEMALE BEAUTIFUL

What makes a female attractive to males? Is it just an overall pretty face, attractive eyes, lips, skin tone, figure, hair, manner of dress, talents, walk, talk or personality? Certainly all of these things, collectively and individually, cause males to be attracted to her, for some she may not look attractive enough, to others she's the things dreams were made of.

THE FRAGRANCE

Have you ever passed by someone wearing an appealing fragrance and suddenly there was an ambience that captivated you to the point where you forgot where you were or where you were going? I'm talking about the kind that puts conversations and thoughts on hold, taking you to a beautiful place, a memory of a springtime where the weather was just right and you, like the air, were filled with love and joy being totally intoxicated by wonderful possibilities. Sometimes it was feelings of innocence, simplicity, peace and "everything's beautiful in its own way." It is similar to the ambience of sheer loveliness the loveliness of a female that has *"The Fragrance."*

What makes a female attractive to males? As we said earlier there are many things, *but two of the most attractive attributes a woman can possess is her femininity and self-confidence (which I define as a love and respect for herself coupled with a strong dose of self reliance and a solid sense of direction). These qualities, in combination, make "The Fragrance!"* When a woman has the Fragrance she is most attractive to a male. It is then that she's her most sassy, sexy, alluring and winsome. He loves seeing her, talking to her, being acknowledged by her and simply being in her presence. There is something about a woman who has the Fragrance that supersedes everything else. She doesn't need to be overly sexy or anything. She could have just come out of the backyard wearing a jean skirt, wrinkled blouse, and gloves with dirt on her face and she would still look great!

Males are acutely aware of a female who has the Fragrance. They may not know what it is or what causes it, but they know when it's there. It doesn't matter whether it is their mother, sister, the old woman who lives across the street, or their wife; to them she is simply a beautiful woman to be admired.

"The Fragrance" doesn't cause males to have lust for a female; it just gives her the embodiment of an appealing aura. However, in respect to romance, a man that first meets a woman in this state instantly realizes that she doesn't need him but he certainly needs her. Notice I didn't say want? A woman can want a male without really being in a state of extreme desperation (we males sometimes call needy/clingy). When she has "The Fragrance," she is not at all clingy or needy. She has this air of confidence that says, without words, how special she is and that it would be worth the while of any male who would take the time to invest in having her in his life to do just that. It says, "I am a female of great value, worthy of being pursued for I am a woman that is going somewhere and not one that is just marking time looking for someone to rescue me."

This air of confidence is not egotistical but a level of comfort with being herself that causes everyone else to realize that there's something quite appealing about her. Anytime you value yourself it favorably affects the way others see you; you are inadvertently teaching others how to treat you. She is confident yet she is approachable enough to make him feel comfortable talking to her. Can you now see how a female who loses this wonderful sense of self literally becomes less attractive to the male in her life? It is not that she becomes unattractive in the literal sense but less attractive from a spiritual and emotional perspective which has a great influence on their relationship as well as what he sees physically. It is comparable to a female beginning to lose respect for a male who loses some of his manhood. In her eyes, he becomes less attractive. When she has "The Fragrance" it will draw more attention than a change in hair color and more glances than a "painted on" dress. It is sort of like the statement made in the movie *A Color Purple*, "she can attract bees without honey and catch a fish without a hook."

Have you ever noticed a female who may not be wearing attractive clothes and not intentionally acting in a manner that would draw male attention but can't seem to keep them away from her? She's got "The Fragrance." If you think she's attracting an audience now, don't let her dress it up. Actually a female that has it can't figure out what she's got. If you ask her she couldn't tell you, so sisters do go around hating her. Don't go around calling her names just let it go. Remember it's not the clothes or anything exterior, it's "The Fragrance." When "The Fragrance" is within, it enhances everything on the exterior, including her smile, skin, hair, shoes, clothing, jewelry and whatever accessories she may have. In other words, "The Fragrance" causes her stock to rise.

Many women wonder why the so called unattractive woman can easily hold a man while the so called fine and foxy women can barely keep one. One of the reasons is that the so-called ugly woman is very feminine and another reason is that she knows how to make him feel good about himself when he is around her. She listens to him and builds an atmosphere that is safe for him to communicate with her. She has the confidence of a woman who feels good about herself which also makes her most attractive and appealing. If you have a lady in your life that fits these qualifications, then you need to buy, build or find a pedestal for this woman and place her there immediately. In fact, you need to give the Lord Jesus Christ some long overdue praise for this woman, regardless of whether she is your mom, aunt, sister, cousin, friend, fiancé or wife. The Fragrance is modest, meaning she has just enough. Not too much of this and not too little of that. This is the state of a woman who has herself and a little something special called "The Fragrance!"

ENHANCED FEMININITY

Now that we have laid out what truly makes a female beautiful I must also say that I am aware that somebody is going to misunderstand it. Some are going to think that as long as they have "The Fragrance", they will not need to do any further grooming. That is not what I am suggesting at all. In fact, a female that has "The Fragrance" has been doing some of these very things on her way to possessing it. How many of you have felt better about yourself whenever you've come from the beauty parlor with a new hairstyle? Didn't you walk with a little extra pep in your step? When your nails were manicured and groomed don't tell me that it didn't affect the way waved at people, handled items and pointed at things. You know good and well it affected how you thought about yourself. Let's not even talk about getting a facial, losing weight or putting on clothes that enhance your assets. All these things enhance your femininity and as we have said when femininity is enhanced, beauty increases. In case anyone is wondering, size does matter! Some guys feel a woman has to have some meat on her bones to be beautiful and others feel that if she's thin she's in, while there are others who feel that she must be voluptuous. In other words don't lose your mind over your size and shape unless it is just something you want to do because there is someone out there who loves the shape and size you're in.

Let's talk about skirts and dresses versus pants. Forget the discussion and let's get right to the point. A female in a dress or skirt is much more appealing than one in pants. Why? It is because it enhances the air of femininity and there's nothing finer than a feminine female. Enough said!

Thinking Highly
One of the best things you can do to enhance your femininity is to think highly of yourself. It is very attractive and when you find yourself thinking that way you exude that feeling to others. It is almost infectious. I know some of you are thinking that I am talking about being carried away with yourself, but that is not at all what I am advocating. To better illustrate what I am suggesting I have included the following "Insight For The Soul" newsletter from 2004 entitled "Making It To Highly."

Making It To "Highly"

Romans 12:3 *"For I say, through the grace given unto me to every man that is among you, not to think of himself more highly than he ought to think, but to think soberly, according as God hath dealt to every man the measure of faith."*

Ephesians 4:1 *"I therefore, the prisoner of the Lord, beseech you that ye walk worthy of the vocation wherewith ye are called."*

Romans 6:18 *"Being then made free from sin, ye became the servants of righteousness."*

Some of us read the above scripture and assume that we should not have a high opinion of ourselves, when the truth is, before you can get to MORE HIGHLY you must first get to HIGHLY. Referring to ourselves in terms of being unworthy, filthy rags, unfit, nothing in us being good; we mistakenly think that we are displaying humility and meekness. What's sad is we do this even after we've been washed in the precious blood of Jesus. This type of thinking greatly hinders our holy walk by subconsciously giving us excuses for living ungodly lives and causes us to settle for being less than we are. You know, a filthy sinner can't help from sinning. We are no longer servants of sin! The scripture teaches us that we are the righteousness of God, a holy nation, royal priesthood, chosen generation, peculiar people and of course sons of God. We are not attempting to cause anyone to become an egomaniac, but we are certainly encouraging you to live up to the standard of our given place in this world. The object to thinking HIGHLY of ourselves is to make living a life of sin something that is beneath us, repulsive, shameful and an insult. We are "The

Light Of The World" and given that responsibility we need to attune our thinking about ourselves so that we can carry ourselves in the proper manner. Some will say that this is a lot of pressure, but it only becomes pressure when you don't think of yourself properly. As a man thinketh in his heart so is he. Let us, for our sake and the cause of Christ think Highly!

SECTION THREE

MAINTENANCE

CHAPTER SEVEN

MAINTENANCE NEEDED
"AN OUNCE OF PREVENTION"

Let's move on to a discussion about how to prevent the female from losing herself. I'm not talking about prevention to the point of her never experiencing the loss of self again, but the prevention of her going there too soon and too often. We want to address this by talking about keeping our relationships growing. In respect to keeping the relationship growing some adhere to the idea that "if it aint broke don't fix it," but when it comes to male-female relationships waiting until it broken is not a good idea. The reason for this is by the time you decide to stop neglecting the relationship it may be too late. It is far wiser to preclude it from getting to that point by doing the routine maintenance when necessary. To this end, we can establish some practices and assimilate information that will not only help her in that area but also help build a deeper and more meaningful relationship with her.

THE BASICS

As we have been saying throughout this conversation; females expect males to instinctively know some things. These things are basic to every relationship and, thereby, essential for communication. Since the female is born with the gift of communication and usually begins to do so earlier than males, to her, in most cases, these things are quite obvious. Don't forget she was created to help him and was given the ability to automatically perform and understand basic communication skills. Unfortunately some males are not always keenly aware of these basic needs that a woman has for communication in spite of the fact that they are sometimes viewed as common courtesies. Most often males find out about them through teaching or sad statements from females such as, "Why can't you be more romantic?" and "You don't show your love for me."

Defining "The Basics"
The Basics are ways of letting the female know that you care, appreciate, notice and are in tune with her that are not dependent on special days (birthdays and holidays), moments or events and does not appear to be timed, rehearsed or calculated (in a negative way). The Basics are done "just because."

You Care: She needs to know that she matters to you. It is important for her to know that she is a priority to you.

You Appreciate Her: Since a female's instinct is to give much of herself to the male, she needs to know that what she brings to the relationship is something that you are grateful for as opposed to something that you are using like a dirty rag. It is important to let her know, in little ways, that you are thankful for all that she does. She actually thinks that this is something that you should be doing as a matter of common courtesy. And you know what? She is correct. Unfortunately, some things have to be taught and when males realize what they need to do believe it or not good ones tend to make the decision to do them.

Let's get a little more practical with this. If the female in your life has worked hard all day, then take some of the responsibilities that she usually takes care of off her hands. If she normally cleans off the table and washes the dishes, then you do it before she even gets a chance. If she normally cooks and you know how, then you do the cooking and clean up the kitchen allowing her to relax and wind down. Take her out to eat instead. Compliment her for the things she does for you. Simply say, "thank you."

<u>You Notice Her:</u> When she does something different she wants you to be aware of it. For example, she wants you to notice that she's changed her hairstyle, is wearing a new outfit or has fixed your favorite meal.

<u>You're In Tune:</u> Getting in tune with the woman is important in a male-female relationship. A woman has a natural desire to be in tune with her surrounding. She can tell the difference in the cry of a baby, the barks of a dog and even the purr of a kitten. She knows whether it's an emergency, he needs water or the cat simply wants to go outside. She is able to distinguish the same type of thing when her baby cries while many of us males just think the baby is crying. It is important that, over a period of time, we should know some of her likes, dislikes, what makes her smile, what it takes to make her happy.

Let me give you a couple of simple examples. One brother bought a huge five-pound box of candy for his wife when she would have been quite satisfied with a simple card and a small box of candy. Don't get me wrong she was grateful for the gifts, but was somewhat disappointed that he didn't understand after all those years that they had been together he didn't realize that she would have been satisfied with less. Another brother bought a bouquet of roses (two dozen) to his fiancé. She took them, said thanks and put them on the dresser. What was wrong? Did she not appreciate the fact that he did a good thing? Believe me, she was happy that he brought the roses, but he never told her why he bought them. In her opinion she would have preferred one rose if he would only tell her why he was giving it. (By the way, we always need to tell them why we are giving them something otherwise they become suspicious and think that we've done something wrong.)

Please do not think that either of these females was ungrateful for what was given. They were extremely thankful for what was done, but at the same time felt that their mates were totally out of tune with them resulting in them feeling a little less important to him. I know it may sound a bit confusing, but take my word for it. Things will work out much better if you take heed. Whether you realize it or not, she is not trying to be difficult. It makes her feel so good inside when you know exactly what she likes and do something that reflects it without her telling you to do so. This tells her that she truly matters in your life. What we are not saying here is that you need to be totally controlled by her. Females do not want males in their lives that they can completely rule. As I've said before, they sometimes want to see the manhood in you stand up. What we are saying is to care enough about the person that you literally take the time to truly get to know them enough to be aware of their ways, moods and changes. Are you going to know all of them or get it right every time? The answer is an emphatic NO! However, you will get it enough to make the relationship more special. This may sound as if it is only for romantic relationships, but the same basic principles apply for females who are family members.

Dads, do this with your daughters and you will begin to discover an awesome relationship developing. For those of you who are wondering why I am not telling the female these things; I want to let you know that if she gave you this book it is because she has already read it. In other words the message has already been delivered to her. Again I want to emphasize that this is not very difficult at all. It only takes a simple decision to pay a little more attention. Here are some tips on how to get in tune with her?

A)   First recognize that there is a need to be in tune with her.

B)   Take a self-inventory. Am I doing the same things I did to win her? If not what am I no longer doing?

C)   Read books and magazines that helps you in those areas.

D)   Sharing and discussing this book with her can do wonders to help you get in tune

E)   Make yourself aware of her "WHY DON'T WE'S" (Note: Ladies you must add a task to it or it will be perceived as a hint and may not get done)

F)   Be attentive, seek to learn her moods, learn when to step in and give her a hand and finally learn some of her likes and dislikes.

G)   Allow time for her to talk to you and listen attentively to what she says. Pay special attention to what she doesn't say and especially watch her body language.

Being in tune with the female is a connection on a spiritual and emotional level that is necessary for proper balance in the relationship. You both need to know where each other stands and feel on a variety of things. It is like best friends that spend a great deal of time with each other. They don't have to guess what the other will do in a tight situation because they are in step or shall we say in tune with each other. When you realize that the female was created as a helpmeet, then you can further see why this is necessary. Surely one cannot be an adequate help if they are not familiar with what your mission is.

Just Because: Sometimes you'll hear a female say that she wishes he would do something "just because," or for no reason at all. Please don't let this confuse you. Doing things "just because" does not mean that there is not a reason; to the contrary, "just because" has a myriad of reasons and incidentally can also bring about a myriad of blessings and benefits. Examples of things you may do "just because" include:

- you wanted to make her smile
- you wanted to remind her of how important she is in your life
- you miss her
- you simply wanted to show her you care
- you are proud of how far she's come
- you recognized she was going through a difficult time
- you wanted to hear her voice
- you were simply having a moment that day
- you wanted to express how you feel
- you wanted to spend some quality time with her

Now that we've defined what we call the Basics let us now take a look at some practical things that can be done which would be considered doing the Basics. (Please remember that these things do not have to be done every single day, but should be considered a normal part of what you do within the relationship. I want to also reemphasize that these things are done outside of special days or moments and are not rehearsed, timed or calculated. They need to at least appear to be on the spur of the moment.) Having made that statement; I need to bring clarification to the idea of it being timed, rehearsed or calculated. What we referring to by planned and calculated is when someone is trying to be deceptive and using this as a tactic to deceive as opposed to using them as tools to better the relationship. The truth is setting up a great event or even a special surprise cannot always be done in the spur of a moment so we are not excluding the planning of something special. The following are a few examples of what you can do:

- Do the dishes if she normally does them
- Bring home something she likes (something as simple as a candy bar) and let her know you were thinking about her (literally say it)
- Call her while you are away from her and tell her you simply missed her and wanted to hear her voice
- Open the car door (or any door for that matter) and let her get in first
- Ask her how her day has gone and actually listen to her for as long as she wants to talk
- Draw her a nice bath with all of the amenities
- Leave her a greeting card or for that matter a personally written letter of appreciation in an obvious place
- Pull out her chair at the dinner table and seat her before you eat your meal
- Fix things around the house that are broken without her asking
- Tell her you love her on a regular basis
- Hug and squeeze her while telling her how much you love her
- Compliment her

- Notice and Let her know you like any change she has made (hair, new dress, fixed the living room etc)
- Take her out on a date (believe it or not you can do this for your mom, sister and even your daughter. It's a lot of fun and she'll appreciate it.)
- Make yourself available to her in times of need
- Applaud her accomplishments
- Mail her a letter (even if you live at the same address) expressing your feelings towards her (don't put a return address on the envelope)
- Become acquainted with her hints
- Allow her to help you without feeling like she's invading your space.

Note: *Guys what I am about to tell you is EXTREMELY IMPORTANT! Please don't ever forget this! Whenever you give a female anything for goodness sake ALWAYS TELL HER WHY! The reason should always be that you love her, you were thinking about her or you knew that she would love to have this. And "I love you" is what she really wants to hear.*

Results from Doing The Basics

Depending on the type of the relationship and how they are perceived or received; The Basics may lead to Philia, Eros or both. Philia is what we commonly call brotherly love. Eros is romantic love. So if you are doing the basics with grandma you could expect to become closer to her in a familial type of way but if this is your wife, girlfriend or fiancée you could expect to have greater feelings of romance present. However, you need to be careful of doing the basics with the wrong female because the message you are sending may not be the one you want sent. Since I was brought up with the old fashion notions of being a gentlemen believing that ladies ought to be respected; I have found myself in a world of trouble. There are times when you need to keep your compliments to yourself. Leave "The Basics" for your relatives and make sure you're careful even when practicing them with them. There are a host of other benefits afforded you as a result of simply doing these basic things:

Competition

After interviewing an endless amount of females and asking them what could possibly result from males doing just "The Basics," I have found that most of them would view it as a competition. What do I mean? Well according to the numerous females that I've spoken to they've said that if someone would do all of that for them that they would in turn do as much or even more for him, not allowing the male to out do them. You see they feel that they invest a lot in their relationships already and usually don't get half as much back. So to receive "The Basics" from a male would be completely overwhelming and would for certain move them to do even the more for him.

More Eros

As stated earlier, Eros is romantic love. If you are in the type of relationship where romance should be present and it is not, then one of the things that is missing for certain is "The Basics." Every female that I spoke to told me that if the male in her life simply did "The Basics" it would totally boost the points for romance in their relationship 100%! That's right I said every female. [As a quick note, here let me tell you that romance (for women) is everything that is done that leads to sex as opposed to most men where it is the sex.] In the eyes of the female, sex is the end result of romance.

"The Basics" can lead to romance and romance can lead to other things. Let's see, what would that amount to? For those of you who are in a romantic relationship and have not been getting enough cuddling, loving and attention. I have just one basic statement to make. It's on the way. It's On The Way. IT'S ON THE WAY!

More Philios
By simply doing "The Basics" you can revolutionize your relationship with your sister, mom, cousin, aunt, grandmother, niece or daughter. Sometimes this is just the thing to rebuild or develop the relationship you've always wanted with them. Through that you will be able to discover things about each other that you never knew, experience things you never imagined and feel about each other what you never thought possible. Yes, Philios can develop to the point that forgiveness and restoration can take place. Who knows what kinds of opportunities it will bring. Only God himself knows what blessings will occur.

Better Communication
We have talked about the lack of and difficulties with communication between the sexes to the point of exhaustion. By learning how to be in tune with the female and exercising the other elements discussed in this chapter, communication with one another is greatly enhanced. Guy through this we are setting the mood and are beginning to hit homeruns. In fact, we are scoring some major points here in the communication area.

Why He Doesn't Do The Basics
The question is: Why doesn't he do the basic "common courtesy" things that are essential to relationships? The problem is that it is assumed by females that he knows to do them. This assumption is a bad one because everyone

doesn't have common courtesies. Our world is not as well adjusted as we would like to think and basic social graces are not being passed on they way they used to. Think about it. Our newspapers, television, magazines and Internet have inundated us with stories of people who are dysfunctional for a myriad of reasons. What we have to realize is that these are things that have to be taught. There was a time when social graces, respect for others and self-respect were taught, but today these are severely missing.

Is it any wonder that there are males who do not know how to treat a female? Of course not, therefore I again appeal to those of us that are mature to demonstrate these qualities in our lives and teach others to embrace them also. Yes I know and I agree that there are those who do know and yet don't do as they should. There are several reasons for this. Let us just talk about at least two of them:

1. <u>Those Who Have Been Hurt.</u> These people have not dealt with their hurts in a proper manner. These people use defense mechanisms which they think are protecting them from being hurt again and don't realize that in order to experience real love they have to open themselves not only to receive this love but also to the possibility of being hurt again. Otherwise, they are simply pushing away those who could possibly be an answer to their prayers.

2. <u>Those That Stop After They Have You.</u> Ladies, believe it or not the reason he stops doing all of the right things after he's got you is that he views them as the tools necessary to accomplish the task of winning you over. He does not see them as tools needed to maintain the relationship. I know it sounds ridiculous but it is true.

He wooed you to win you and when he won you the task was accomplished. Therefore, it doesn't register that the dating, courting and romancing must continue. Ladies, I have some good news for you in spite of this paradox. Males have the ability to make a decision without emotion and actually see it through.

Okay ladies stop the laughing. This is serious business because some of the males in your life are not doing things like telling you that he loves you because you cannot relate to this principle. To add to this dilemma most females will criticize a male who attempts to do the right thing without, what is perceived as, the right emotions behind it. Let me give you an example of this. I counseled a couple that had this very problem. I told the male to make the decision that he was going to say good things to his wife and especially tell her that he loved her every day. Mind you, I said this right in front of the female. I told her not to give negative looks or say anything about how he expresses these things to her. I further explained that he will not initially articulate his feelings with the proper emotion but if she allowed him to practice doing it he will eventually say these things to her the way she needs to hear them. I told her to take as it comes and accept the compliments. I admit it wasn't easy for him but she was patient and now he says and does things with the emotion and passion that her heart desired. What am I saying?

First off, he views the basics as only a tool to win you and secondly that he can turn this around by making the decision to commit to using them to continuously build the relationship stronger while learning how to do it with the passion, articulation and emotion that you need. Brother I believe right now that you want to make that commitment. Come on let's do it right now.

Dear God, I bring myself before you knowing that you are able to help me better my relationship. I, thank you for giving me these tools to know what to do and empowering me with the wherewithal to see it through. Therefore I, from this day forward, commit myself to doing the Basics in my relationship with my wife (sister, mom, aunt, grandmother etc) and am determined regardless as to what may come or go to become the man that you intended for me to be in Jesus' name. Amen.

TAKING CHARGE

Females love it when a male has direction and is able to take charge of a situation. They don't like the idea of having to always tell males what to do and how to do. She takes great pride in you handling these things without her insistence. Let's not forget that she was created as a helpmeet and not someone that has to constantly tell him what to do. As we said earlier she likes it when he takes the initiative. This does not mean, however, that she wants to be totally left out of the decision making process but it does mean that she expects a male to be capable of making a decision and taking total responsibility for it. For example, she would love for you to do something as simple as decide how the two of you will spend the weekend by taking the initiative of making all of the arrangements. The fact that he does not ask her to make the arrangements gives her the feeling that he can handle things for her and is not always dependent on her to figure things out.

Here's another little tidbit that I must share with you. Brothers, it is extremely important that you sometimes say no to her request. Females love that. I know this does not make sense but in spite of how she may complain and protest, she would like for you to stand up to her and say no. Don't be a jerk about it but understand that this is part of how she determines your manhood. She wants to know that she has a man and not a mouse. Please understand she doesn't want you to be harsh to her but only wants to make sure that you haven't totally gone soft. Believe me she will be expecting you to continue treat her in the manner she has grown accustomed. Females need the steel and the velvet.

Here is a situation that I have found to be a common one. Whenever there is not enough income to pay the bills it is extremely important for the male to take charge and get this handled. First of all you must always have a plan to take care of the situation. Secondly you must always show and explain the plan to the female so that she can see that you've got things covered. Let me tell you something. You don't ever want a female to think that you are not capable of putting together a solution to handle your financial problems to the extent that she will have to do it herself. This has been the cause for numerous difficulties in relationships. She needs to see the plan and know exactly what you propose to do and are doing. If you just let her handle and pay the bills without the funds to do so, then you are not protecting her femininity. You will cause her to worry. You see men tend to shelve things while the female is still thinking about them long after the experience is over. So to prevent her from worrying too much while you are yet handling the situation, take the bills from her and make the arrangements to pay them yourself until you are at a point where there is enough to easily pay them. Thirdly, if it takes getting a second job, do it. Don't ask her opinion on this. Just go out and get it done and don't return until you have gotten everything paid up with some extra funds to spare. Don't worry about her wanting you to be home for now because if those bills aren't paid you are going to wish you did. When you've handled your responsibilities, you can then come home as her man and her hero. Believe me she will applaud and respect you for it.

Mothers please make sure that you teach your sons to take the initiative. Do not expect him to automatically know this. Be very specific when you are telling him how important this will be in his relationship with the females in his life. Sometimes they are not able to get this from the males in their lives and even if they do your reinforcement is very important. Brothers, please assimilate this information as you read this book. If this doesn't make sense to you take some time to discuss this with a female that you feel comfortable with. You may be quite surprised. If nothing else brothers I want to leave you with this, it will keep your lady from being vulnerable to a real man.

YOUR RELATIONSHIP AFFECTS OTHERS

Brothers, please understand that your sons and daughters are greatly affected by your relationship with their mother. One of the greatest things you can do for your children is to love their mother. Your daughter indirectly learns what to expect from a male when she treats him as a good woman should by how her dad treats her mom. She also learns how to treat a good man by the way her mom treats her dad. The same principle applies to sons.

Do you really want your daughter to expect the male in her life to treat her as you have treated her mom?

My wife told me of an incident where my son was looking at the price on the box of chocolates I had purchased for her. Yes, they were Godiva for those of you who had to know! He said "Daddy paid this much money on a box of chocolates for you?" She looked at him with a smile on her face that spoke of the wisdom only a mother could possess and said "don't you think I'm worth it?" To which he replied with the realization that there was much more to it than the actual cost of a box of chocolates "Yes mom. You are worth it!"

As his father, I had taught him by my actions and without words that I valued his mother very highly. The same principles apply to mothers. Mothers, one of the greatest things you can do for them is to respect their father. Listen, even if that man is a total bum and has left you alone to take care of those children with no financial, moral or emotional support, do not bad mouth him in front of or to his children. When you destroy his name you also destroy your children for they identify themselves with him. In time they will recognize him for what he is without your help but, for now, you need to refrain from disrespecting him in their eyes and ears. There is so much more that I can say about this but for now I want you to simply pursue your relationship's growth and enjoy it knowing also that as you are being blessed so are others who are observing from the sidelines.

DAD HELP YOUR DAUGHTER(s) THROUGH INFATUATION:

My Aunt Margree told me many years ago that a male has not lived until he has had a daughter! Of course at the age of 16 I was in no way form or fashion interested in having any children, much less a daughter. However, her words were to become words of great wisdom and blessings to me in the coming years when I finally became the father of two beautiful little girls. Daughters have a special place in the hearts of their fathers and no male, regardless of how wonderful he is, can ever be good enough for his little girl. Nevertheless fathers mature to the point that we realize that they cannot remain our little girls forever and never seem to rest until she has someone that will love and take care of her as much as we have.

When this happens we relax a little and are not as overly concerned about her welfare. With this thought in mind I want to help dads better the chances of the proper guy coming into her life while deepening the relationship the two of them already have by helping him walk with her through her feelings of infatuation. Once we settle in our minds that they are going to fall in love, let us take an active part in her experiencing those crazy emotions we commonly refer to as being in love. Guys we all know the dangers but sometimes don't know how to be a part of it. We know that she needs us more than ever at this point but we also know that she probably doesn't want to talk to us about it. Being aware of all of these things, we need to do some work in advance of this happening. Enjoy talks with your daughter and when she begins to hit puberty don't run away from her or your feelings that have tremendously grown at that point. Yeah that's right. Now that she has reached puberty you have become more passionate towards her. Just so you know what's going on and to put you at ease; you are not in love with your daughter! It is nature's way of letting you know that she will be leaving in a few years and that you don't have much time left to help her in some of the remaining lessons on relating to the opposite sex. You are, and have been, her role model for what she should expect from a male. It's transmitted through the way you treat her and how you treat, respect and respond to her mother. It's well documented fact that women who have had healthy relationships with their fathers are more comfortable with who they are and are more capable of choosing right relationships with the males in their lives. So the passion you feel for her is a great thing! Just be her dad.

It is important as a dad that you walk through it with her when she experiences infatuation. Let her know in advance that you know that this will happen and when it does you want to be there for her. Your daughter needs for you to be a soft place for her to land. She also needs to know that it is all right for her to have these feelings and that she should enjoy the experience. Let her express her giddiness, while helping her to understand that she should not immediately express them to the object of her affection. Remind her that she has no idea where any of this will end up but to enjoy each moment in the safety of anonymity. Respect her feelings; don't make her feel stupid. She's already feeling terribly confused as it is. If she is acting sort of silly, just realize that she isn't doing this with his (whoever the joy killer is ☺) knowledge. Laugh and enjoy this time with her until she comes to the place where she can finally see him with some clarity. In doing this you will protect your daughter and also enrich the relationship you already enjoy as well as giving her insight as to how a male should treat and respect her. By the way dads, you inevitably will have this "pleasure" several times in a daughter's life so if you've messed it up the first time apologize and let her know that you want to walk with her through it. I realize it may not sound like a great thing to some, but when you've experienced it you'll know that it was well worth it.

The following is an insert from my teenage daughter Jenise

FATHERS SHOULD BE A SOFT PLACE TO LAND AND A HARD ROCK TO STAND ON

After doing an extensive review on experiences of my own and of my friends, I've come to the conclusion that every young woman has to learn how to have a real relationship. We all had to go through, or rather have a relationship where we kind of "lose ourselves." We sacrifice ourselves, our time, our bodies our belongings, our family, and just us as a whole. Sometimes we sacrifice ourselves and the results are extremely destructive but other times we pick ourselves right back up without any serious damages. To God be the glory, I walked away unharmed but in other cases, women give themselves and the only way to get it back is to surrender to Jesus! And to think, all of this is a tie in with daddy.

At the age 17 or 18, when young women start dating more seriously, fathers are in most need. Our fathers determine what kind of woman we'll become, the kind of men we choose, the amount of confidence we have, the type of relationships we develop with men (sexual or otherwise), and the amount of respect we have for ourselves as well as others. Most women look at their fathers (or father figures) as a guide to what their mates should be like. I read a book where the protagonist's father was a major drug dealer. He smothered his family with money, clothes, jewels and anything they could imagine. He wanted them to have the "finer things" in life. He set some good morals in his daughter but he mostly lit the fire to her hunger for money and things that eventually led to her imprisonment. The men that she considered to be potential mates were in some way or another tied to drugs. I was saddened by the story because the girl was filled with riches but deprived of goals and a vision to get more out of life. Her mind was so small and limited. She devised many plans in the story to get what she needed to be done but the one plan she didn't devise was the one that would get her out of her tenement building (project) mindset and into the real world. Her father's influence (as well as her own choices) landed her in a cold prison cell. That's why so many of our black men are out on the corner instead of a corner office somewhere in Manhattan.

You know whenever I see these young men and these drug dealers on the street and they try to talk to me I just want to tell them, " You need Jesus first and your daddy second." I never realized how much my father meant to me until the Lord opened up my eyes. At this time the decisions I make in life are critical. This is my transformation from girl to woman and my father's guidance will help decipher all of that (and no doubt Jesus).
Between the ages of 16 and 21, young women should be discussing sex, dating, goals, desires and their vision for life with their father. I know sex is a touchy subject but it is necessary that we get his input, outlook, insight, and everything else. His wisdom on the subject will really open our heart and mind on what direction we should go in and what decision we should make. If we could grasp hold to this information, I think we'd be a much better people.

DEPENDABILITY + TRUST = VULNERABILITY

One of the things that we want to make women aware of is their vulnerability to what appears to be a dependable man. We also want to inform good males that they need to protect this vulnerability in their female relatives. One of the most important things females desire in a male is that he simply be someone upon whom she can depend. In many cases, the male that she is with may not be as aware of this need as he should be, so for his sake we want to help him become keenly responsive to this requirement. For many men, fixing something around the house is not always a top priority but for the woman it is very important. Leaving the house broken for her is like leaving herself broken or undone. In other words it becomes personal and not something that is just an inanimate object sitting in the home. It gives her a sense of wholeness and security when the male handles things in a timely manner or at least let's her know when he plans to take care of it. Of course if he makes a schedule of when he is going to actually fix things he needs to keep his word. In fact it gives her a feeling of comfort and confidence when he handles things without her ever having to tell him at all.

This is part of what she means when she says that she wants him to be a man. Basically, she is saying that she wants him to be responsible, to take the initiative in doing things that need to be taken care of and to be able to make decisions. When the male is not aware of this or fails to handle this responsibility and another male consistently steps into this place; the male in her life is leaving her vulnerable to the possibility of infidelity or possibly placing her in a position where she will begin to question his manhood. This doesn't have to be verbal. She can simply stop asking you to handle certain things and do them herself. This is not good because whenever a female has to look past you it becomes not just a matter of dependability but also matters of trust, which is not an easy thing to get regain. There are many males whose wives (or other women in their lives) have taken the reigns and are not willing to trust him to handle his position as the male or man in her life. As we said earlier women desire to have a male that they can depend on.

The story of Joseph (Genesis 39:1-19) gives the best example of how this can happen. While Joseph was a slave in the house of Potipher, he became supervisor over everything that they owned. He made sure that all the needs of Potipher's family were met kept a record of everything they produced and brought great wealth to his masters. According to the scriptures his master didn't even know how much money he had. As a result of this Joseph was not treated like an ordinary slave. He wore the best clothes and in the eyes of the entire household Joseph was the man of the house. Now it must be understood that Joseph never flirted with Mrs. Potipher, but in her eyes he was the man in her life. Why, you may ask? It is because he was the one who met her needs on a consistent basis and through this she became quite comfortable with him causing her to see him in a totally different light. His motives were honorable but that didn't matter to her. Her husband had allowed her to become vulnerable and she let herself feed into this fantasy to the point that she was ready to force Joseph to have sex with her.

Now let us go over some lessons that cam be learned from this episode. Brothers, make sure that you are aware of the need for a woman to have a male that she can depend upon. Secondly, protect her and yourself by taking care of your responsibilities and finally be careful of being so helpful to other women who are not relatives for you are not quite as strong as you think. Sisters, true to the Eve Factor this is something that is innate so you need to make yourself aware of it. You also need to be aware that some men are not conscious of this, so if you have a husband, son, boyfriend etc. you need to clearly warn him. You need to spell it out for him in plain old English. You need to get him this book! Don't beat around the bush. Tell it like it is. For both males and females please be aware that there are males and females that are experts at this and are looking for opportunities to capture prey. The way this works is simple. First there is Mister Helpful, then trust is built and over a period of time someone gets too comfortable. That's why the formula is DEPENDABILITY + TRUST = VULNERABILITY.

CHECK THE GAUGES

Relationships are like some of the old furnaces with lots of gauges. Those gauges must be monitored and if one of them is off, then the engineer has to adjust the gauge to keep the furnace running properly. Just like the furnace relationships have gauges too and when just one of them are off it creates problems in the relationship. Gary Smalley (*Hidden Keys To Loving Relationships 1993 Tape 2), famed relationship author, taught that there are five areas within every relationship that are necessary for healthy relationships. When I say necessary, I mean if they are not set as they should the furnace will explode and destroy the entire house. I call them gauges.

There is the Security-Gauge, Meaningful-Communication-Gauge, Basics-Gauge and the Physical-Contact-Gauge. Whenever something is wrong in the relationship you can be sure that one of the gauges is of out of balance. Throughout this book we have in one way or another referred to and addressed each of them. I have listed them below, to remind and inform you that they are primary to the success or failure of our relationships. If you understood nothing else that I have said please know that it is up to us to make sure that we maintain a proper balance of these gauges for the optimal health and life of that which we treasure most dear and that is each other.

Security-Gauge: Security in a relationship is that the other person is committed to love and be there for you regardless of what it takes and what happens.

<u>Meaningful-Communication-Gauge:</u> This is simply sharing your feelings and can very well include things like how your day actually went.

<u>Basics-Gauge:</u> I think you've guessed this one. Practice those things listed under the Basics in this very chapter.

<u>Physical-Contact-Gauge:</u> This includes a warm embrace, holding hands, leaning on one another, a kiss on the forehead and any meaningful touch between family members.

CHAPTER EIGHT

PAIRING

Can two walk together, except they be agreed?
(Amos 3:3)

If you learn nothing else from this book, it is my hope that you have learned that we need each other and that we all have value to bring to the table of our familial associations. Take the time to understand one another's strengths and learn how to forgive and have patience with our weaknesses while becoming proficient in knowing how to use them to make our relationships better. Now the question is: how to be a house united. I have given you some tools that I know can help you win the battle in our families. We have the most logical vehicle for togetherness – the family – yet it seems in too many cases we are incapable of maintaining our relationships in bringing a greater fulfillment in our familial involvement.

FATHERS AND DAUGHTERS

Its true good dads love and cherish their little girls without regard to how old they become; they are always daddy's little girls. When this relationship is properly brought together it is one of the most rewarding and greatest experiences a man can have. Men that develop a proper relationship with their daughters experience a fulfillment that's comparable to very few things. Fathers gain a sense of pride knowing that he is the one his daughter will come to when she needs a strong shoulder to lean on as opposed to the nearest male that makes himself available to her; realizing that such a male may or may not treat his daughter in a manner befitting her. Understanding that he, in her view, is what a man should be makes him want to be a better man. That sense of pride also speaks to the feeling of fulfillment a dad has when he knows that he has done his job as a father. Generally, we fathers do not feel that we can rest until our daughters find someone that will love and take care of them as we would. However, knowing that our relationship is good brings a sense that she will have the proper judgment and know that she won't have to seek out things in any other male that which only a father can give his little girl. The unconditional love and confidence that a daughter has in her dad is one of the most satisfying, ego boosting elements of the relationship; it is called hero worship. To earn it he doesn't have to be the greatest, most handsome, smartest or strongest guy in the world. He just needs to be her dad. It causes his chest to swell, smile to broaden and his feeling of generosity to open wide as she wraps him around her little finger. Yeah its true dads are sometimes weaklings (or as some of you moms like to put it, suckers) to their daughter's desires. Why? Because they have a special place in his heart and daughters know how to love up on their dads and boost his ego. And dads love it! (In fact they revel in it.) I want to tell you first hand that having my daughters in my life going through all of the changes good and not so good is one of my greatest joys. To go from being their idol, becoming the blithering idiot and finally becoming the man of great wisdom and knowledge (although they might say that slightly different) has certainly been a journey worth taking. It has not been an easy journey but the men out there that have committed themselves to being good fathers can attest to the fact that there are very few things like having the love or their daughters.

Being able to listen to their concerns, requests for advice and desire to share special moments of success and aspirations can't be measured by any amount of currency! Sometimes we laugh about them and believe it or not they are quite grateful that I loved them enough to give them special time. They are not half as grateful as I am for the privilege. Everything has not always been good between me and my girls but when they were not as they should I determined in my heart to love them in spite of disagreements, pursue them when necessary, pray for them when we were apart and allow them to grow as individuals while learning to respect them as young ladies. I believe this has allowed us to have the relationship we enjoy today. It is a relationship that is worth everything it took to obtain.

My girls sometimes say that I am mushy, but when it comes to a man's daughters, as hard as it is for us males to admit, we go there. The relationship is not without a daughter's benefits. As told by my daughter Jenise, dads need to be a soft place for them to land and a hard rock to stand on. Every well-adjusted female that I have known has benefited from either a strong relationship with her father or a solid father figure. Much of their self-esteem is affected by their relationship, or lack thereof, with their fathers. There's something extra special that takes place in her when dad believes in her. It seems that there is a sense of security given within that relationship and when it is not there she seems to look for it within the male that she becomes involved with leaving her a little more vulnerable than she should be. She also receives that unconditional love and attention so necessary for her personal growth. Daughters thrive and abound when their dads love them just as they are, unconditionally. It gives her a sense of well being and fills the void that no other male can generally fill in her life. He is that protector, leader and provider and one of the greatest encouragers she can have. A female with a dad who believes and encourages her has a beauty within her spirit that permeates everything she does.

While it is obvious that this relationship fosters great familial benefits it can also produce great business relationships and of course lasting friendships. Take for example John Johnson and Linda Johnson Rice; they are better known as the owners of the multimedia conglomerate Johnson Publishing Company that publishes *Ebony*, *Jet* and historical books (like *Before The Mayflower* by Lerone Bennett Jr). They also have highly successful broadcasting, fashion show (Fashion Fair), hair-care and cosmetics divisions, including Fashion Fair Cosmetics, the No. 1 Black-owned cosmetics company in the world with 2,500 stores on three continents.

Mr. Johnson founded the company in November 1942, with a $500 loan on his mother's furniture and has groomed and turned over the duties of President and Chief Operating Officer to his daughter Linda Johnson Rice in 2002. She graduated from the University of Southern California's School of Journalism and in 1987, earned a master's degree in management from Northwestern University's Kellogg Graduate School of Management. Two days later she was named president and chief operating officer of her father's businesses, Fashion Fair Cosmetics and Johnson Publishing Company. Today the company is worth $350 million and employs 2,000 people[1] (www.johnsonpublishing.com). You must understand that this is no arbitrary choice made by Mr. and Mrs. Johnson, for you don't just simply turn over that kind of empire to your child when there has been no proven relationship that included trust. This is a relationship that has been cultivated over many years and is culminating in even greater trust between this father and daughter relationship. If you had the opportunity to speak to Mr. Johnson about his daughter or Ms Johnson Rice about her dad you will find that the love, pride and passion they both have for each other would totally overtake them as their faces beam with the most precious of memories. Fathers and daughters deserve to have the privilege of a loving association.

MOTHERS AND SONS

This is what seems to be the easiest of the relationships to maintain. How many athletes have you seen waving in the camera with the words "hi mom" on his lips or after receiving an award thanking his mom? The pride of a mother is a son who has grown up to be a solid productive man. One of the problems with this, like dads and daughters, is smothering him to the point where she doesn't allow him to grow into independence. However, I want to encourage females to fight for this relationship especially those of you that feel like there are not many good men in the world. You have the greatest opportunity to change that. At the same time, you can have the most wonderful relationship with someone who will always look out for mama. Mothers are the greatest cheerleaders in a son's life. When everyone puts him down, she will take on the entire world for him. She is the first woman he falls in love with and the one who teaches him how to treat a female. Sons, you will never find, outside of a good wife, anyone who will love you quite as much.

Your mom will literally walk through fire to rescue you. She is the one who will stick with you long after the male responsible for your being born has left. When he has long since given up on taking care of you, she is the one who will care for you regardless of the price she has to pay. She'll eat tuna and crackers for weeks just so she can afford to put you into a good school. Don't forget that she put herself at death's door to give birth to you. It was a grateful son who wrote the song "I'll Always Love My Mama"; a song that I am sure speaks the personal sentiments of Jonnetta Patton's son, Usher Raymond.

Jonnetta, a single mom, and her son have formed an incredible relationship while also propelling him to the top of the entertainment industry. As his manager she has helped her son gain a broad spectrum of acting, singing, writing, performing and producing[2] (Ebony September 2004 pg 188). In 2004, this mother-son team received what seemed to be an endless amount of nominations and awards for his album Confessions that set sales records throughout the year.

In the area of ministry, Ms Dodie Osteen has encourage and worked with her son Joel, who was a cameraman for their ministry's television department, to the point where he has not only stepped into his father's shoes, the late John Osteen, but has taken the ministry to another level while turning himself into a world renowned preacher.

BROTHERS AND SISTERS

The relationship between brothers and sisters is the relationship with the greatest opportunity for male-female friendship. Not burdened by the complexities that romantic associations bring or the obligations of parenthood, it is free to explore all of the possibilities that a committed friendship can bring. Think about it. Who knows you better and has a more natural desire to be connected with you than your sibling? Whenever they are able to forge pass rivalries and the desire to push each other's buttons and learn how to forgive past wrongs we will find that there is a natural desire to see the best for each other. There is a natural sense of protection and partnership that has the ability to flow effortlessly. I know there are quite a few siblings reading this with frowns and other negative looks on their faces, but in spite of that, who but your sibling will literally go on the attack if anyone but them is doing you wrong? I tell you when siblings decide to work together on a given project there is the potential for great things to happen and if you are honest with yourself you will see that I am right.

I have three sisters, one of which is deceased. My youngest sister and I seem to have always been rivals but I have the most wonderful memories of us helping one another when we both were down. I also have a fantastic memory of us working together to plan and execute a party to show our mom how much we appreciated her. I suppose you may be wondering why I used the word execute. It is because we teamed up with such precision that made it made it more than just a job well done. My sister was masterful! I enjoyed working with her so much that I would gladly volunteer to do it again. I recognized her strengths as well as my own and throughout the project allowed her to do what she did best while doing what I was best at doing. Needless to say everyone, especially mom, had an awesome time. In fact, there were those who attended who knew neither our mom nor us and said that they never felt such a feeling of love at a family event.

The relationship of siblings, believe it or not, can work very well for business relationships too. One of the things that we need to learn is when it is proper to be a mama or poppa to our sibling and when it is not. If we can learn how to separate this and also respect each other's roles there is the possibility for great success. Actress-comedienne Monique, of the television series "The Parkers," who has successfully parlayed her accomplishments into the area of a fashion line for full figured women and added show hosting to her resume, has nothing but praise for her big brother who has taken over the reigns as manager. According to Monique, he has taken a lot of pressure off of her and is doing an excellent job looking out for his sister[3] (www.1monique.com).

The Versace siblings, Gianni, Donatella and later older brother Santo, build an enormous fashion house. Relying on one another's strengths instead of criticizing each other's weaknesses, they established themselves as one of the premier designers in the world. From the start of his career, Gianni consulted his sister in his most important decisions, and Donnatella's bravura and dedication made her integral to Versace as the company grew[4] (www.versace.com).

HUSBANDS AND WIVES

There are several types of relationships between males and females but the ultimate relationship, in my opinion, is that of husband and wife. It is within that relationship that we see the greatest potential for God's blessings and original plan (Genesis 1:26, Proverbs 18:22, Proverbs 31). I call it God's success vehicle in the Earth. Husband and wife can, and really need to, be best friends, lovers, business partners and anything they choose. It is an awesome opportunity that can actually work better than a charm. When they are armed with the proper information and the commitment to the relationship there is no stopping them.

Bishop TD and Serita Jakes, for example, have taken the favor (Proverbs 18:22) of their marriage and friendship into every endeavor afforded them. They've created highly successful ministries, multimedia businesses that include film, plays, books, music and an outrageously successful Mega-Fest event that combines all of their flagship ministries ("Woman Thou Art Loosed" and "Man Power") with activities that minister to the entire family and community. You've got to realize that part of Bishop Jakes' God-given revelation on women had to come from and/or complemented by his wife, Serita. This is another example of a couple who were able to learn their strengths and how to use them to the betterment of themselves and finally others.

UNCLES AND NIECES/COUSINS

This relationship, when done right, can be similar to or complement to the father-daughter relationship. There is no better example of this than the story of Esther and her uncle-cousin Mordecai, found in the Book of Esther. When her parents passed away he took her in and raised her as his own daughter. She was brought up in a loving home, taught social graces and was exposed to the finer things in life. When a decree was put out that the King sought a maiden to become the Queen, Mordecai showed his confidence in her and insisted that she had everything it took to take advantage of this wonderful opportunity. He made her feel good about being a female and gave her the self-assurance that she could be not just a beauty queen, but also a real queen. Her mannerism and personality enhanced her beauty to the extent that when she went to the palace she gained favor, receiving the best of preparations for purification and finally impressing the King to the point that she was without competition. The funny thing about kindness given to someone is that you never know how it will come back. As it turns out Mordecai's encouragement of Esther in becoming Queen resulted in her rescuing her entire nation from certain genocide.

AUNTS AND NEPHEWS

This can also be a substitute or even complement the mother-son relationship. I have personally been quite fortunate to have been blessed with some aunts who have given me encouragement, wise counsel, love and comfort when my mom was, for one reason or another, unable.

Two are better than one; because they have a good reward for their labour.

For if they fall, the one will lift up his fellow: but woe to him that is alone when he falleth; for he hath not another to help him up.

Again, if two lie together, then they have heat: but how can one be warm alone?

And if one prevail against him, two shall withstand him; and a threefold cord is not quickly broken.

(Ecclesiastes 4:9-14)

EPILOGUE

And Jesus knew their thoughts, and said unto them, Every kingdom divided against itself is brought to desolation; and every city or house divided against itself shall not stand:
(Matthew 12:25)

I have taken quite a bit of time to think about what I want to say to you, now that you have taken the time to finish reading this book. My deepest desire is that you do a few things for yourself, your family member and of course me. If you are a female, I would like for you to take time to simply love you. If you have found that you are lost, take time for replenishment and give you back to yourself knowing that we all miss your wonderful self. Secondly, I want you to learn from whatever lessons there are in this experience while forgiving yourself and others.

If you are a male, I want you to have the ability to truly love the female in your life appreciating all that you both bring to the relationship table. I also want you to share what you have learned with one another for the conversation will bring a deeper level of communication and increase the possibility of finding the hidden treasure.

I suppose you are wondering what I am requesting for myself. If it is at all possible I would like for you to not just read this material, but to internalize it. I want you to learn from it. I also want you to share it as you receive results and help others to do the same. Finally I would like for you to share your stories with me. Tell me what helped you the most. Visit my website and email me (www.stevewaltersministries.com). What is this book really about? It is all about family. If you use what I have shared with you I sincerely believe that we can, as a result reduce child abuse, the occurrences of single family homes, the divorce rate, crime, the amount of women being abused, the suicide rate, the need for anti-depressant drugs, the occurrences of dysfunctional families, increase optimal health, better our schools and neighborhoods.

So please don't just read this book. Use the contents and share with someone else making our world a little bit better for us all. May God be with you and Heaven smile upon you.

Yours in Christ's service,
Bishop Steve B. Walters

ABOUT THE AUTHOR

Steve B. Walters is founder and president of Steve Walters Ministries a national outreach dedicated to providing the finest biblical teaching, tools and training to empower and enrich individuals to be Spirit filled, self-sufficient workers for Christ. He shares from practical first hand experience of how believers can apply the Word to the circumstances of life and live victoriously. He is the author of "Receiving The Holy Spirit: With The Evidence Of Speaking In Tongues", "A Shepherd's Journey: Life Story Of Apostle Lymus Johnson", a newsletter entitled "Insight For The Soul" and numerous tracts and pamphlets. Steve's televised appearances include guest spots on Atlanta Live Show (Channel 57) and the "Jesus" Show (People's TV, Atlanta). He is also a regular guest on "Can We Talk" (Cable show in Brooklyn BCAT and Manhattan). Steve and his wife Sharon live in Atlanta, GA and have three children and three grandchildren.

For further information on books and other ministry items visit his web site: www.stevewaltersministries or e-mail him @ Bishop@stevewaltersministries.com

ML

8/0